FRANCIS FRITH'S

AYR - A HISTORY CELEBRATION

CW00507810

THE FRANCIS FRITH COLLECTION

www.francisfrith.com

AYR

A HISTORY AND CELEBRATION
OF THE TOWN

ROB CLOSE

THE FRANCIS FRITH COLLECTION

www.francisfrith.com

First published in the United Kingdom in 2005
by The Francis Frith Collection®

Hardback edition 2004 ISBN 1-84567-739-0
Paperback edition 2012 ISBN 978-1-84589-696-6

British Library Cataloguing in Publication Data

Ayr - A History and Celebration of the City
Rob Close

The Francis Frith Collection®
Oakley Business Park, Wylye Road,
Dinton, Wiltshire SP3 5EU
Tel: +44 (0) 1722 716 376
Email: info@francisfrith.co.uk
www.francisfrith.com

Printed and bound in Great Britain
Contains material sourced from responsibly managed forests

Front Cover: **AYR, HIGH STREET 1900** 46002t

Additional modern photographs by Rob Close.

Domesday extract used in timeline by kind permission of
Alecto Historical Editions, www.domesdaybook.org
Aerial photographs reproduced under licence from
Simmons Aerofilms Limited.
Historical Ordnance Survey maps reproduced under licence from
Homecheck.co.uk

Every attempt has been made to contact copyright holders of
illustrative material. We will be happy to give full acknowledgement in
future editions for any items not credited. Any information should be
directed to The Francis Frith Collection.

Contents

AYR FROM THE AIR 1972 AFA222839

Historical Timeline for Ayr

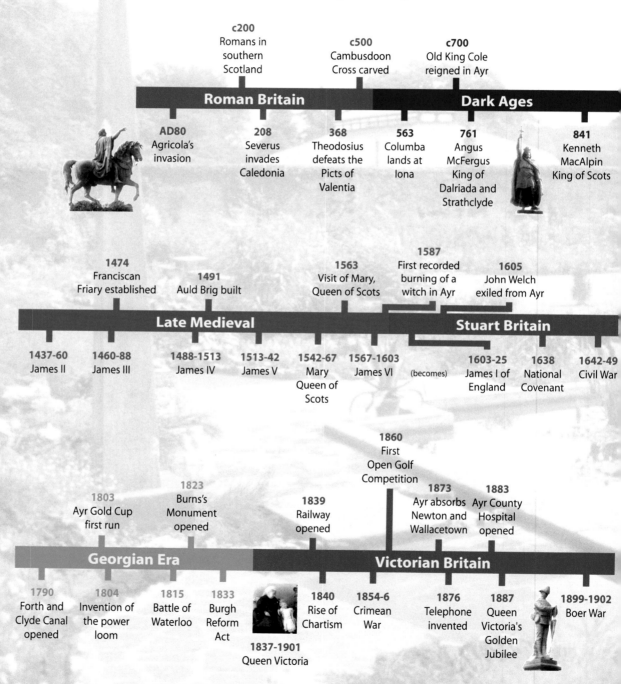

c200
Romans in southern Scotland

c500
Cambusdoon Cross carved

c700
Old King Cole reigned in Ayr

Roman Britain

Dark Ages

AD80
Agricola's invasion

208
Severus invades Caledonia

368
Theodosius defeats the Picts of Valentia

563
Columba lands at Iona

761
Angus McFergus King of Dalriada and Strathclyde

841
Kenneth MacAlpin King of Scots

1474
Franciscan Friary established

1491
Auld Brig built

1563
Visit of Mary, Queen of Scots

1587
First recorded burning of a witch in Ayr

1605
John Welch exiled from Ayr

Late Medieval

Stuart Britain

1437-60
James II

1460-88
James III

1488-1513
James IV

1513-42
James V

1542-67
Mary Queen of Scots

1567-1603
James VI

(becomes)

1603-25
James I of England

1638
National Covenant

1642-49
Civil War

1860
First Open Golf Competition

1873
Ayr absorbs Newton and Wallacetown

1883
Ayr County Hospital opened

1803
Ayr Gold Cup first run

1823
Burns's Monument opened

1839
Railway opened

Georgian Era

Victorian Britain

1790
Forth and Clyde Canal opened

1804
Invention of the power loom

1815
Battle of Waterloo

1833
Burgh Reform Act

1840
Rise of Chartism

1854-6
Crimean War

1876
Telephone invented

1887
Queen Victoria's Golden Jubilee

1899-1902
Boer War

1837-1901
Queen Victoria

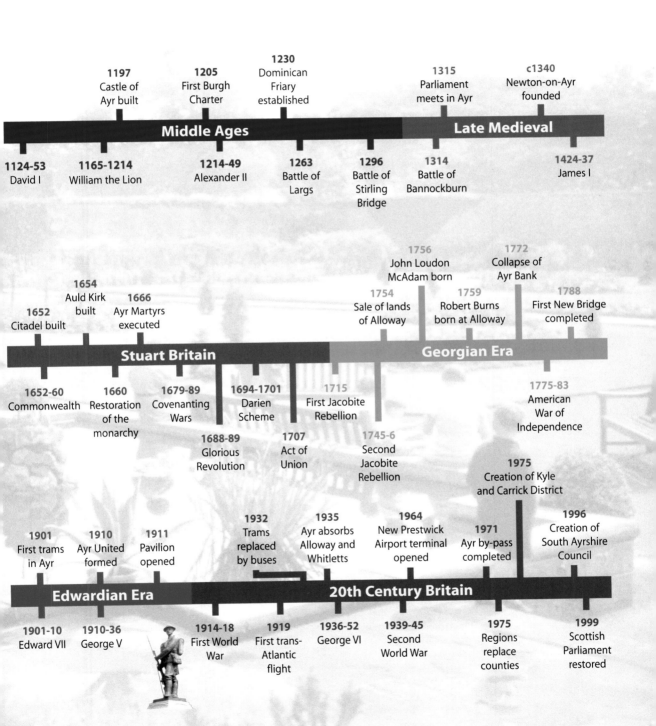

Middle Ages | **Late Medieval**

1197 Castle of Ayr built
1205 First Burgh Charter
1230 Dominican Friary established
1315 Parliament meets in Ayr
c1340 Newton-on-Ayr founded

1124-53 David I
1165-1214 William the Lion
1214-49 Alexander II
1263 Battle of Largs
1296 Battle of Stirling Bridge
1314 Battle of Bannockburn
1424-37 James I

Stuart Britain | **Georgian Era**

1652 Citadel built
1654 Auld Kirk built
1666 Ayr Martyrs executed
1754 Sale of lands of Alloway
1756 John Loudon McAdam born
1759 Robert Burns born at Alloway
1772 Collapse of Ayr Bank
1788 First New Bridge completed

1652-60 Commonwealth
1660 Restoration of the monarchy
1679-89 Covenanting Wars
1694-1701 Darien Scheme
1715 First Jacobite Rebellion
1775-83 American War of Independence
1688-89 Glorious Revolution
1707 Act of Union
1745-6 Second Jacobite Rebellion

Edwardian Era | **20th Century Britain**

1901 First trams in Ayr
1910 Ayr United formed
1911 Pavilion opened
1932 Trams replaced by buses
1935 Ayr absorbs Alloway and Whitletts
1964 New Prestwick Airport terminal opened
1971 Ayr by-pass completed
1975 Creation of Kyle and Carrick District
1996 Creation of South Ayrshire Council

1901-10 Edward VII
1910-36 George V
1914-18 First World War
1919 First trans-Atlantic flight
1936-52 George VI
1939-45 Second World War
1975 Regions replace counties
1999 Scottish Parliament restored

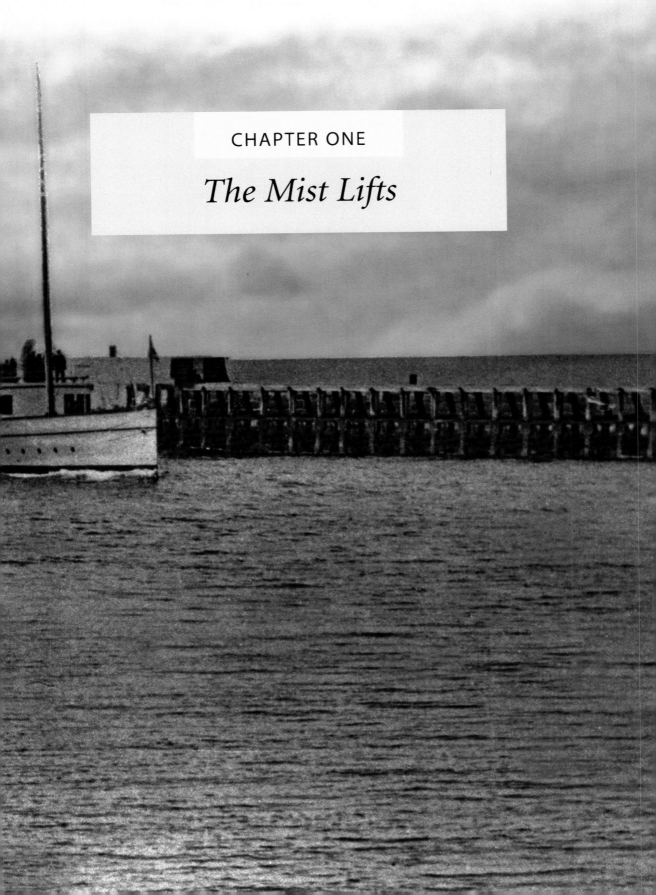

CHAPTER ONE

The Mist Lifts

*'Auld Ayr, wham ne'er a town surpasses,
For honest men and bonie lassies.'*

ROBERT BURNS'S well known distich from Tam o' Shanter has stood as a motto for the town almost from the day it was first composed. For most people, Scotland's great poet is the first person they associate with Ayr, and his honest and sincere tribute to the town brings Burns and the town together, and sets us off on this celebration of Ayr and its history.

A PORTRAIT OF ROBERT BURNS 1897   39858A

Did you know?
What's in a Name?

The name Ayr has never been satisfactorily explained. It was originally applied to the river, and the town was first called St John's Town of Ayr, and the name must have been in use long before it was first written down in the 12th century. Rivers with similar names are found in England (Aire), France (Aire), and elsewhere in Europe. Various meanings have been suggested, such as 'clear river', 'rapid river', 'violent river' or 'shallow river.'

The modern town of Ayr sits on the west coast of Scotland, at the centre of a wide bay in the Firth of Clyde. Into this bay flows the River Ayr, completing its journey from the Ayrshire moorlands above Glenbuck, and as it does so, creating a natural sheltered harbour. In the times of early man, the ground on either side of this river mouth would have been a jumble of sandy knolls, small brackish pools and impenetrable thickets of gorse. The chapters that follow will show how man fashioned this landscape to create the town we know today, but we must begin with those early men.

In the Mesolithic period some 6,000 years ago these sandy foreshores were frequented by fishermen and their families, who wandered among them scratching a bare living from the sea. They had little, and have left little. The few traces of their existence that do turn up, such as flint tools, are dumb witnesses to the daily life of these first Ayrshiremen.

In the Neolithic period, the New Stone Age, a similar itinerant lifestyle would have continued. The development of the stone axe, of which examples have been found in Alloway Street and at Doonfoot, enabled these early settlers to adapt the landscape more readily to their needs.

During the Bronze Age, about 3,000 to 3,500 years ago, these wandering family groups began to settle. There is evidence from many places throughout Ayrshire to show that this area was well populated, and that these people had the ability to grow food. They could store food in earthenware pots, for they knew how to make these, and knew how to make implements from metal. They had also begun to develop what we might recognise as a society, for they honoured their dead, and at least one burial site was found in the early 19th century at Content, on the north side of the River Ayr.

In the Iron Age we move into a period which we can better understand. The Iron Age in Scotland largely coincided with the Roman occupation of southern Britain. Following the conquest of southern Britain, Roman troops attempted to subdue the tribes such as the Picts and the Damnonii, who lived in northern Britain, and who were reluctant to come under Roman rule. The Romans'

18TH-CENTURY PRINT 'TWA BRIGS' ZZZ04144 (Private Collection)

This 18th-century print shows the strategic position of Ayr at the mouth of the river, protecting an important crossing point.

first attempts were unsuccessful, and the Emperor Hadrian decided to withdraw to a defensible line between Carlisle and Newcastle, and built, as a solid evidence of the Roman frontier, the wall which bears his name. His successor Antoninus, however, made a second attempt to subdue the tribes in the south of what we now know as Scotland, and achieved a certain degree of success. At his command a second, more northerly wall was built between the Clyde and the Forth, effectively bringing Ayr within the Roman Empire.

There is little actual evidence of the Roman period in Ayr's history. There was a fort at Loudoun Hill, in the east of the county (near Darvel), and evidence for temporary marching camps has been found at Largs and Girvan. One route which may have been a Roman road, and was certainly believed to be so in the 19th century, is that which comes into Ayrshire south of Dalmellington, and runs up the Doon Valley, and then over Cockhill and into Ayr past the site of the new Ayr Hospital, and seems to be making for Castlehill. Castlehill, too, is a name which suggests that there was some form of camp or fort.

After the Romans withdrew from southern Scotland, the historical record again becomes fragmentary. This is the period known, with good reason, as the Dark Ages. The people who lived in this part of south-west Scotland, the Damnonii, became part of the kingdom of Strathclyde, ruled from the royal seats at Dunadd and Dumbarton, both north of the

THE PIER 1896 SA000056 (Courtesy of University of St Andrews Library)

An unidentified paddle steamer is seen entering the harbour in 1896. The shelter provided by the river mouth was an important element in the development of Ayr from earliest times.

The Scots

At the time when modern Scotland was occupied by the Picts in the north and the Celtic Damnonii and others in the south, the Scots, who spoke Gaelic, lived in Ireland. It was only in the period after the collapse of the Roman Empire that the Scots began to move to Scotland, where finally they became the dominant force.

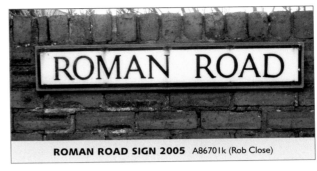

ROMAN ROAD SIGN 2005 A86701k (Rob Close)

This street name was first used in 1959, despite opposition from some councillors who doubted its historical accuracy.

Clyde. Perhaps because of their position on the coast, these people were in contact with other peoples, such as the mysterious Picts to the north, and the Gaelic-speaking Scots in Ireland.

From these years, folk history and communal memory bring down to us a few half-probable and fabulous events. They have the spurious accuracy of urban myths, but may, at heart, contain the germ of a truth. In AD360 there was, we are confidently told, a battle on the shore between Ayr and Doonfoot in which a combined force of Picts and Romans defeated an army of Scots. In 681 another army of Scots were driven from Strathclyde after being defeated by the natives at a battle near Mauchline.

Besides these threats from Ireland, the people of Ayrshire were also to find themselves targeted by Vikings. The first Viking raid into the Firth of Clyde is recorded as having occurred c870. The Vikings were to prove a constant threat until 1263, when the Norse King Haakon was decisively defeated at the battle of Largs.

Invaders, too, came from the east. In 750 the Northumbrian King Edbert took control of much of Kyle, and perhaps was able to bring some prosperity and the Northumbrian brand of Christianity to the area. It is noteworthy that churches of Prestwick and Kirkoswald are dedicated, respectively, to the Northumbrian saints Cuthbert and Oswald.

During this long period, we can see Ayr and its neighbouring territories as being fought over by these different tribes, each struggling to carve out a territory for itself. Into this complex mix we can now add Christianity. As already seen, the Northumbrians may have brought their form of worship from the east. From the south and west, however, were to come the missionaries from the Celtic church who were to do much to shape early Scotland.

We do not know who the first missionaries to Ayr were, nor when they came. Some early missionaries to Ayrshire are recorded in place names, such as St Winning at Kilwinning, and St Marnock in Kilmarnock, but the brave soul who first preached in

Ayr must remain anonymous. He, or his successors and followers, have left one clue. A large stone, with a carved cross, found at Cambusdoon and now in the Loudoun Hall has been dated by one expert to the period between 30 and 500.

The mist of the Dark Ages begins to clear after AD1000. During the 10th century Strathclyde and Lothian, in the east of Scotland, were combined into one kingdom of the Scots. In 1066 William of Normandy defeated the English at the Battle of Hastings. While this did not immediately affect life in Scotland, the ripples would eventually reach into the northern kingdom. In 1114 a list was made, and written down (and it still survives!) of the lands belonging to the bishop of Glasgow. Three of these places were in or close to Ayr: Sanchar (modern

St Quivox), Camcachecheyn (the farm o Camsiscan in the parish of Craigie) and Carcleuien (Carcluie near Dalrymple).

The 12th century saw the consolidation of Scotland into a single recognisable unit largely Christian in belief, under three kings David I, who reigned from 1124 to 1153, hi successor Malcolm IV, and William the Lion who came to the throne in 1165. Much of thei success in subduing outlying areas, such a Ayr, was because they recruited generals and soldiers from amongst the Norman nobilit who had helped William to conquer England From these Normans sprang families such a the Bruces and Stewarts who have done s much to shape Scotland's history.

Under these kings and their Norman generals, the area of 'secure' Scotland wa gradually extended, until in the south

Did you know?

Was This Camelot?

One of the most persistent fables concerns the legendary King Arthur. It is said that he was in this area leading a roving army band, bent on driving invaders, probably the Scots, out of Britain. He had his headquarters on the headland where later Greenan Castle was built, and this has been identified by some Arthurian scholars as the site of Camelot. This early 19th-century view of the castle shows the growing town of Ayr in the distance.

A 19TH-CENTURY VIEW OF GREENAN CASTLE ZZZ04145
(Courtesy South Ayrshire Libraries)

only one area remained outwith the king's control. This was the lordship of Galloway, which included Carrick (southern Ayrshire), the borders of which reached to the River Doon. Wooden castles - mottes and baileys - were built to defend Scotland from the earls of Galloway. Two survive at Alloway and at Dalmellington. Hostilities between the two continued, with each taking the upper hand on occasions. In 1160 Fergus, Lord of Galloway, was deposed by a military expedition led by Malcolm IV, but while William the Lion was held prisoner by the English in 1174, Galloway reasserted itself. It was again conquered in 1177, but in 1196 Fergus's grandson Roland again threatened Scotland. In 1197 William the Lion built a new royal castle at Ayr, and by playing 'divide-and-rule' was able to win over Carrick to his side, and in 1207 Carrick was incorporated into a new sheriffdom (shire) of Ayr, with Kyle and Cunninghame.

A Merry Old Soul

The nursery rhyme hero, Old King Cole, is thought to derive from the semi-legendary King Coilus, who was a leader or princeling, paying tribute to the kings of Strathclyde. Coilus is supposed to have been involved in the battles to keep the Scots out of Strathclyde, and, the story says, died in a battle with the Scots King Fergus, near Dalrymple. A cairn near Tarbolton is known as King Coil's Grave. The name Coilus is believed to exist in the place names Kyle (for that part of Ayrshire which has Ayr as its centre) and the village of Coylton.

THE CAMBUSDOON CROSS ZZZ04178 (Author's Collection)

This precious early Christian relic was found in 1929 and is now on display in the Loudoun Hall.

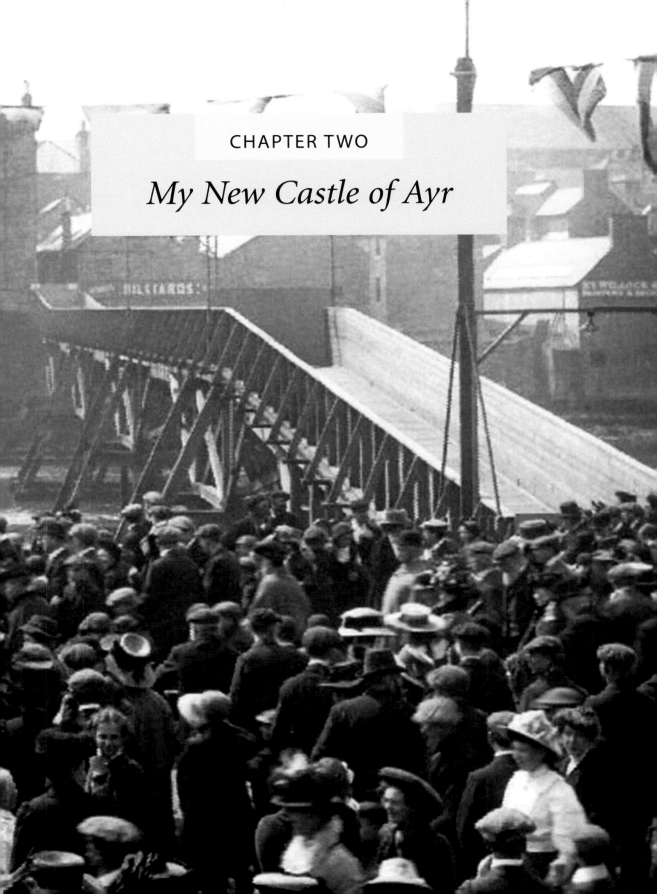

CHAPTER TWO

My New Castle of Ayr

'My New Castle upon Ayr'

William the Lion's castle was a wooden keep on the sandy hills to the south of the river mouth. From this position it could guard against threats from the sea, and watch for approaches from the dangerous, unconquered, Galloway south. The wooden castle was replaced by a stone castle in 1307. This, too, had been abandoned by the 17th century, and all trace of it was destroyed when the fort of Oliver Cromwell's troops was built in the 1650s.

The illustration shows an imaginary representation of the castle, issued as part of a series of postcards.

COAT OF ARMS POSTCARD
ZZZ04146 (Private Collection)

ON 21 MAY 1205, King William the Lion was in Lanark with his closest and most trusted advisers. They had important work to do, for William was to sign the charter creating a royal burgh at Ayr. This signal honour showed that the town outside William's castle had begun to grow in status and importance. It had many important advantages. It lay close to the castle. It had a good and safe harbour. It was at a ford across the river. Within two years, it had a sheriff, and had taken the first steps towards becoming the town we know today.

It also had a church. This was built just outside the boundaries of the town, and lay between it and the castle. Its tower still survives, and has witnessed many tumultuous events and suffered many vicissitudes.

This photograph of 1946 demonstrates Ayr's strategic position on the south bank of the river. The view is dominated by the town steeple.

THE RIVER AYR WITH THE MODERN BRIDGE 1946   SA000069 (Courtesy of University of St Andrews Library)

The Low Green

William's charter granted to the town of Ayr a large common land south of the town. Much of this land, which was originally used for grazing animals and drying cloth, has gradually been built over. The Low Green, which provides a valuable green lung close to the town centre and is also hugely popular with visitors, is all that survives. In its present form it dates from 1894, and covers about 45 acres.

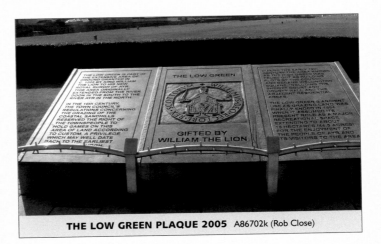

THE LOW GREEN PLAQUE 2005   A86702k (Rob Close)

William's new town attracted traders, and it attracted churchmen. In 1230 the Dominican monks were encouraged to come to Scotland by the king, Alexander II, and he established eight monasteries for them, of which one was at Ayr.

The Dominicans wore black robes, and were commonly known as the Black Friars. They saw their mission as one of preaching and converting people to the faith. Within the grounds of their monastery in Ayr was a well, St Katherine's Well, which was highly regarded as a source of health giving water. The Black Friars remained in Ayr until all monasteries were dissolved in the 16th century.

The earliest development of the town was along the road which led under the castle and church, from the ford over the river (approximately where the New Bridge is today) and continuing on towards Carrick and Galloway. This is the street we know as Sandgate. Perhaps this area was always too much at risk from the sands blowing off the dunes, for as the town grew a second, and finally more important, street developed at right angles to Sandgate, and running roughly east and south, paralleling the river. This street had two advantages. It was less at risk from wind-blown sand and, importantly in a sea-trading town, it gave half the people of Ayr direct and private access to the river, with wharves where they could moor their boats. This street is the one we know as the High Street. These two streets, Sandgate and High Street, with their origins in the mists of the early 1200s, are still the heart of Ayr. In the settled years of the early 13th

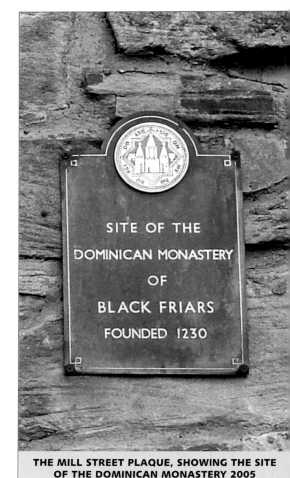

THE MILL STREET PLAQUE, SHOWING THE SITE OF THE DOMINICAN MONASTERY 2005
A86724k (Rob Close)

century the town consolidated. In 1236 there is the earliest written reference to a bridge over the river. This was probably a wooden bridge, possibly the first of many (for storms and spates are not unknown in Ayr) that preceded the Auld Brig, the first stone bridge, built in 1491.

Threats to Scotland's stability came from within and without. In the years before the Battle of Largs, when there was a real threat of invasion by the Vikings, Alexander III

The medieval parish church of Alloway was in regular use until the 1690s.

came to Ayr to personally supervise the defence of the castle and the construction of new ships. A generation before this the lands of Galloway and Carrick had threatened to rebel, but the crisis had passed, and Ayr's part in this was recognised by generous grants from Alexander II in 1236.

In 1286 Alexander III died, without an obvious successor. Seeing a leaderless Scotland, Edward I of England seized the chance to extend his influence, and invaded Scotland in 1296, forced the king, John Balliol, to abdicate, and imposed English rule on the country. The Scots were not impressed, and the country plunged into the Wars of Independence, culminating in defeat for the English at Bannockburn in 1314.

**THE STATUE OF WILLIAM WALLACE,
NEWMARKET STREET** ZZZ04147 (Private Collection)

**THE STATUE OF WILLIAM WALLACE,
THE WALLACE TOWER 2005** A86703k (Rob Close)

These two 19th-century statues of William Wallace are in Newmarket Street and on the Wallace Tower.
Many people must pass them daily and not be aware of their existence.

The first true leader to emerge to fight the English was William Wallace. Wallace was born around 1267-1270, possibly in Ayrshire, where the Wallace family owned land at Ellerslie in Riccarton. Certainly many of the early stories of Wallace place him in Ayrshire, as when he single-handedly fought with five English soldiers near Riccarton. He, it is said, escaped from prison in Ayr by feigning death, and there are many Wallace's Caves locally where he hid while conducting his guerrilla campaign against the English.

After Wallace was captured and executed in 1305, Robert Bruce emerged as the leader of the Scots. He, too, had powerful connections with Ayr, for the Bruces had become earls of Carrick in 1272, and Robert Bruce was

born at their castle at Turnberry in 1274. It was from Turnberry and Carrick that Bruce began the final campaign in 1307 to oust the English from Scotland. His first successes were in Glentrool and at Loudoun Hill, both in 1307, and in 1314 he claimed the culminating victory at Bannockburn.

Did you know?

Parliament in Ayr

The first meeting of the Scots parliament after the victory at Bannockburn was held in the Church of St John in Ayr (St John's Tower). The king and parliament, anxious to avoid the uncertainty of a disputed throne, agreed on a line of succession which was adhered to, and which, in 1371, saw Bruce's grandson, Robert II, succeed to the Scots throne. He was the son of Bruce's daughter Marjorie and her husband Walter the Stewart, and the first of the long line of Stuart kings and queens of Scotland, and ultimately of England also. The picture shows the church during the time it was occupied as a house by 'Baron' Miller, a wealthy local character.

ST JOHN'S TOWER ZZZ04148 (Private Collection)

The Barns of Ayr

During the wars between Wallace and the English, the gentry of Ayrshire were lured by the English to the castle of Ayr, where they were captured and hanged. Wallace, in retribution, surrounded the barns in Ayr where the English soldiers were billeted, set the barns ablaze, killing the occupants, and escaped to a neighbouring hill where he watched 'the Barns o' Ayr Burn weel'.
The hill today is called Barnweil Hill, where there is a 19th-century monument commemorating Wallace and his exploits locally.

A YOUNG BOY 1900 46002x

Trade and commerce have always been vital to Ayr's prosperity. John Wregg had a fishmonger's business on the corner of Mill Street from 1893 until 1929, and there was a fish shop here until 1970.

Ayr, meanwhile, continued to grow and prosper. A small settlement had begun to develop on the northern bank of the river, close to the old ford and the new wooden bridge. This was called Newton-upon-Ayr. It was outside the boundaries of the royal burgh and, therefore, was free from some of the restrictions on trade and commerce which the burgh charter contained. It would have attracted a migrant community, keen to take advantage of the economic opportunities which the royal town and burgh offered. Newton, it is claimed, provided 48 men to fight with Bruce at Bannockburn. As a result, the little settlement was made into a burgh in its own right, while the 48 men who had been at Bannockburn were made the first Freemen of the burgh, with rights and privileges which their descendents enjoyed into the 19th century.

Did you know?
Bruce's Well

At Kingcase, between Ayr and Prestwick, is a well known as Bruce's Well. There was a small leper house here, to which Robert I, who suffered from leprosy, came for treatment. The well was restored in 1912.

BRUCE'S WELL 2005   A86704k (Rob Close)

In the succeeding centuries Ayr developed as the county town, especially as a settled group of landed nobles came to the fore: families such as the Kennedys, Montgomerys, Cunninghames, Crawfords and many others. Each had their estate and tower house in the country, but many also built comfortable town houses in the county town. They needed to be in Ayr to take part in the administration of the affairs of the county and in the dispensation of justice, but they would also have enjoyed the opportunities this offered for social events and leisure pursuits.

In 1474, Ayr gained another monastery when the Franciscans, or Greyfriars, settled in Ayr, where Pope Sixtus IV, who commissioned the Sistine Chapel, gave them dispensation to build a 'habitation with church, altars, a little belfry, dormitory, refectory, cemetery and gardens.' The site they were granted, at the heart of the burgh, may have been the site of an earlier chapel. After the monasteries were dissolved, the site was used in the 1660s to build a new church for Ayr.

The site that was granted to the Franciscans was just above the wooden bridge. In 1491 this was replaced by a stone bridge, the one which is today known as the Auld Brig. This bridge of four arches made access to Ayr from the north much easier. The bridge was rebuilt in 1588 and was thoroughly restored in 1910 after it had been threatened with demolition

Loudoun Hall

One of the leading families in the county was the Campbells of Loudoun, who had become, around 1400, hereditary sheriffs of Ayr. Their seat was at Loudoun near Galston. In 1539 they acquired from James Tait the imposing house which his family had built, probably in the 1490s, and this became the town house of the Campbells. It was one of the finest of the town houses in Ayr. During the 19th century and early 20th century it fell on hard times, but was rescued from demolition in the 1930s. It was restored after the Second World War, and now acts as a meeting place and home to many of Ayr's flourishing societies.

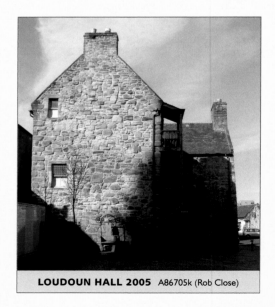

LOUDOUN HALL 2005 A86705k (Rob Close)

The Auld Bridge

Now one of six bridges across the river within the boundaries of Ayr, the Auld Brig was the only bridge until the first New Bridge was opened in 1788. This was the bridge to which, in Burns's poem 'The Brigs of Ayr', the Auld Brig spoke, saying 'I'll be a brig when ye're a shapeless cairn!', prophetic words that came true when the New Bridge was damaged by floods and was replaced in 1877-1878. It is shown before and after its restoration in 1910, as well as during the re-opening ceremony that year. This is still a major gathering point for swans.

TWA BRIGS 1900 46001

THE AULD BRIG, THE RE-OPENING CEREMONY 1910 ZZZ04179 (Private Collection)

THE AULD BRIG, RIVER AYR 1946 SA000068 (Courtesy of University of St Andrews Library)

Ayr witnessed further changes during the 16th century. Some of these were brought about by the suppression of the monasteries during the middle of that century. One important result of that change was that the burgh council had to take more of an interest in education. Teaching would now be in the hands of schoolteachers. This was something that had previously been left to the priests and the church. Records of 1233 mention 'Allan, master of the schools of Ayr', and these schools were presumably attached to the church. In 1559 the council appointed John Orr as the first lay teacher as the children of the town were suffering 'a great hurt … through not having an intelligent and qualified schoolmaster to teach them in manners and the art and science of the Latin

THE AULD BRIG, RIVER AYR 1946 SA000068 (Courtesy of University of St Andrews Library)

tongue and grammar.' The town's new school flourished, and has grown into today's Ayr Academy. A new school building was built in 1602, and this was replaced (on the same site) in 1800, and again in 1880. This building is still in use, though it has been extended and remodelled internally to adapt to changes in teaching methods.

Twice the town was visited by Mary Queen of Scots, firstly in 1552 and again in 1563, when on 2 and 3 August she had 'soupper et coucher at St Jehan d'Era.' It is not definitely known where she stayed, but local tradition has it that she slept at St John's Tower. The century was also enlivened by a series of vicious and bloody feuds that flared up between some of the local landed families and their supporters. Slights and imagined slights led to attacks and revenge attacks that today seem scarcely credible. Ayr was spared much of the horror of the long feud which lasted throughout the 16th century between

Ayr Academy

Ayr Academy is seen here soon after the existing building had been completed in 1880, and a contemporary view of the three heads - James Watt, Robert Burns and David Wilkie, representing science, literature and art.

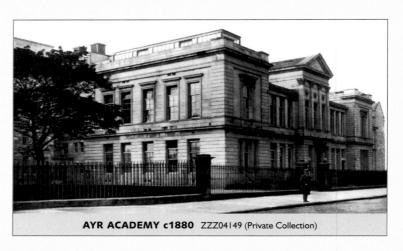

AYR ACADEMY c1880 ZZZ04149 (Private Collection)

AYR ACADEMY 2005 A86706k (Rob Close)

the Cunninghames and Montgomeries in north Ayrshire, but the town saw trouble of its own, as in 1537 when 'great numbers' of Crawfords and Lockharts attacked Alexander Kennedy of Bargany in his Sandgate town house. Crawfords and Kennedys clashed in 1564 at the Tolbooth of Ayr, and again in 1567 during the annual horse racing on the sands of Ayr. The bloodiest and most intense feud however was between two related branches of the Kennedy family in Carrick, those of Cassillis and Bargany. It began in 1570 as both sought to gain the lands of Crossraguel Abbey, with the notorious roasting of the abbot of Crossraguel (a Bargany Kennedy) by the earl of Cassillis, and ended with the coldly calculated murder near Greenan in 1602 of Thomas Kennedy of Culzean by John Mure

of Auchendrane, a supporter of Bargany. This episode, on which Walter Scott based his 'Tragedy of Auchendrane', ended with the hanging of Mure for this crime in 1611.

The old Tolbooth, from which Wallace had escaped and where the Crawfords and Kennedys had met in bloody conflict, was by this time in poor condition. It had stood since the 13th century. The council decided that a new Tolbooth was required, and on a new site, in the middle of the Sandgate, opposite the entrance into High Street. It was to contain offices for the council, a prison, a court room, and was to have shops on the ground floor. It was completed in 1575, and the old Tolbooth removed. The new Tolbooth stood until 1826, by which time it was both unsafe and a traffic hazard.

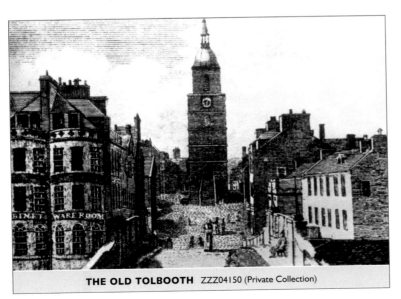

THE OLD TOLBOOTH ZZZ04150 (Private Collection)

When the Tolbooth was demolished the stone was sold to John Robb of Blackburn, who used it in the wall around his property. This included the gallows stone, which could at one time be seen in the wall at Gartferry, a Victorian villa in Racecourse Road built within the Blackburn estate.

THE OLD TOLBOOTH ZZZ04151
(Private Collection)

AYR ACADEMY c1880   ZZZ04149 (Private Collection)

Ayr's trade continued to grow during this period. Transport by sea was still the most efficient means of travel, and Ayr maintained its regular links with Glasgow, London, the ports of Ireland and northern England, and also further afield to France and Scandinavia. The discovery and colonisation of North America and the islands of the Caribbean opened up further opportunities for Ayr. It is not known when the first Ayr ship sailed to America, but by the early 17th century two Ayr merchants, William Kelso and Robert Rolland, were trading in tobacco imported from across the Atlantic.

In 1603 Elizabeth, Queen of England, died and James VI, King of Scotland, became King James I of England. The hundred years between this Union of the Crowns and the Union of the Parliaments in 1707 was a century which saw considerable change in Scotland and in Ayr. It was during this period that Ayr left behind its medieval origins and began to develop into a modern town.

THE AULD BRIG O' DOON 1897 39860

The medieval Brig o' Doon, which carried traffic south from Ayr.

Welch's Garden

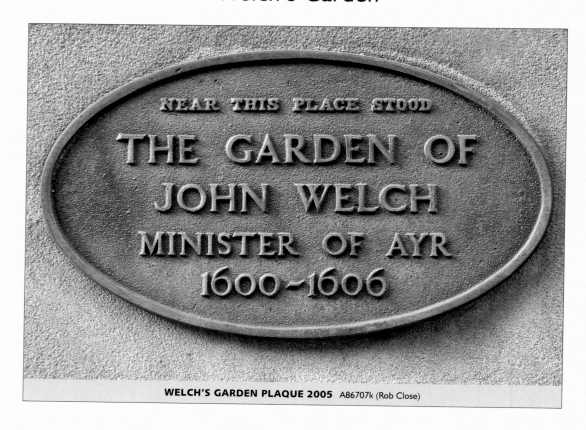

WELCH'S GARDEN PLAQUE 2005 A86707k (Rob Close)

One of Ayr's first Protestant ministers was John Welch. He was born about 1570, at Dunscore in Dumfriesshire, and came to Ayr in 1600. His wife Elizabeth was a daughter of the great reformer John Knox. Welch was a popular and well loved minister, strongly Presbyterian in outlook and, so his followers believed, blessed with the gift of second sight. On one occasion this gift saved the town from plague, when travellers were, on his word, forbidden entry to the town. They went instead to Cumnock, and infected that town with the plague. In 1605 Welch, with other ministers, defied the king, James VI, by meeting secretly. He was arrested, sent to Blackness Castle in West Lothian, removed from his post, and then banished from the kingdom. He went to France, where he remained until his death in 1622. During the 17 years after he was dismissed, Ayr town council continued to pay to him their share of his minister's stipend. His garden, where he regularly prayed, was preserved as 'one of the most sacred and historic places in Ayr' and remained until 1968, when it was lost to progress. A plaque in the High Street acts as the sole reminder of this good man.

Ayr in the first half of the 17th century still had a predominantly medieval outlook. The feuds continued. Superstition and fear were dominant features of everyday life and the exercise of the law. This showed itself particularly in the pursuit and punishment of witches. Witchcraft was made a capital offence by the Scots parliament in 1563, and in Ayr witches were regularly tried and punished. The first recorded occasion was in 1586, when the town council spent £7 3s 8d (£7.18) on the trial and execution of 'the witch of Barnweill'. Others were convicted and punished at regular intervals. The last record was in 1658 when Janet Sayers was convicted, strangled at the stake and burnt to ashes.

The last persecutions of witches occurred during the 1650s. By this time Ayr was in the grip of an English occupation. The complex politics and religion of the 17th century led in Scotland to the Bishops' War (1640-1641), as elements of the church struggled for supremacy. The issue was whether the church should be led from above by bishops (Episcopialian), or from below, with local control at church and local council (or presbytery) level (Presbyterian). James VI and I had been a Presbyterian, but his son, Charles I, who succeeded in 1625, believed in Episcopalian rule, which had become the established norm in England after the Reformation. The Scots were strongly, and proudly, Presbyterian, and Charles's attempts to introduce bishops to Scotland led to conflict and war. In England, Charles's highhanded manner led to conflict between him and Parliament, and to the Civil War, which culminated in the king's execution

> ## Did you know?
> ### *Maggie Osborne*
>
> *Ayr's best known witch was Maggie Osborne. Stories of Maggie Osborne attributed many deeds to her, including raising a storm to destroy ships in Ayr harbour and bringing about a snowstorm to bury someone who had slighted her. She was, it is said, either a tavern keeper or the unfortunate daughter of a good family. No evidence has been found for the existence of a real Maggie Osborne, though a house in the High Street, now demolished, was consistently known as Maggie Osborne's House.*

in 1649. In 1643 the Scots Presbyterians had joined with the Parliamentarians in opposing the king, but were aggrieved when Parliament then reneged on a promise to introduce Presbyterian worship to England.

Charles I's successor, Oliver Cromwell, sought to subdue Scotland, and after defeating a Scottish army at Dunbar in 1650, set about garrisoning Scotland. To do this, he built a number of citadels from which his forces could control the country. One of these was at Ayr, and was built between 1654 and 1656.

The citadel was built on the sand hills on the sea-side of Ayr, where William the Lion's castle and church had been. The church was requisitioned as part of the new fort. Most of it was probably demolished at this time, though the tower (St John's Tower) was permitted to remain as it was an important seamark for vessels approaching Ayr and seeking to locate the harbour mouth.

Cromwell's Fort

Cromwell's fort can still be traced. Most of the strong stone walls, with bartizans at each corner, survive. The top of the main entrance gate can still be seen in a lane off Citadel Place (see photograph A86708k). The powerful walls can be seen easily in many places such as in South Harbour Street and Arran Place. The buildings of the garrison have gone, for the fort or citadel had a lively history after it was decommissioned. In 1663 it was granted to the Montgomeries of Eglinton, one of the big and powerful land-owning families in north Ayrshire. They called it Montgomerieston, and began to encourage trade and industry, in direct competition to Ayr. Industries which were tried at the citadel included soap works, distilling, textile and woollen works and, most successfully, a brewery. In the 19th century the fort was bought by John Miller, a local man who had made his fortune in India. He restored the tower of the church, adding to it to make a home for himself, and began to develop the area within the walls with housing. The fort is still a popular and sought-after residential area.

MILLER'S FOLLY 2005 A86709k (Rob Close)

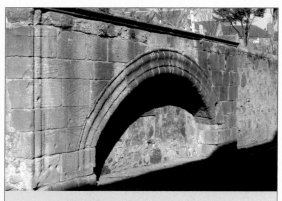

CROMWELL'S FORT, THE TOP OF THE ENTRANCE GATE 2005 A86708k (Rob Close)

One place where the fort wall is very visible is in South Harbour Street. The look-out tower at the corner, however, is not part of the original wall, but was added by 'Baron' John Miller around 1860.

Did you know?
An Ayr Brewer

In the early 19th century Peter Walker was briefly the tenant of the brewery in the citadel. From Ayr he went south and ran breweries in Warrington and Liverpool. The business prospered. Peter Walker and his son Sir Andrew Barclay Walker became wealthy men, prominent citizens of Liverpool, and benefactors of the arts. Sir Andrew gifted to Liverpool its major art gallery, the Lady Walker Art Gallery. Walker's beers continued to be famous into the late 20th century, when the company merged with a big Yorkshire rival to form Tetley Walker.

As a result of the construction of the fort, Ayr lost its church. As compensation, the commonwealth of Oliver Cromwell gave some money (1,000 merks, or about a third of the total cost). A site was found - the site where Ayr's second monastery had been founded in 1474, and a new church was built. This is the Auld Kirk, which survives to this day.

After the death of Cromwell and the restoration of the monarchy in 1660, the garrison of the fort was withdrawn. However, many of the soldiers, and the English tradesmen who had come to Ayr in their wake, remained in Ayr. Some, we know, had married local girls, and had become involved in local trade. Others, perhaps, saw

The Auld Kirk

Ayr's Auld Kirk was built between 1652 and 1654, during the period of Oliver Cromwell's commonwealth. It is one of the very few churches in Britain built during this period. It has been restored and altered on several occasions since, but remains an important reminder of that troubled period.

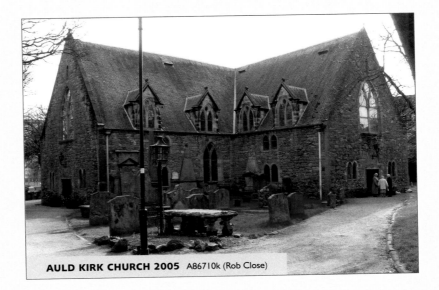

AULD KIRK CHURCH 2005 A86710k (Rob Close)

the opportunities that the town offered. The trading community that developed after 1660, with its mixture of Scots and English talents and skills, began to transform Ayr into a town with widespread trading links, especially by sea. They, the rest of Ayr, and Scotland had, however, to contend with the continuing political and religious unrest. The accession of Charles II had been generally welcomed, but it soon became clear that he was as determined as his father to introduce Episcopalian rule to the church in Scotland. This led to the often bloody and brutal war of attrition between the government and those who opposed this, usually known as Covenanters, from their allegiance to the National Covenant of 1638, which laid down unbending support for Presbyterian rule of the church. The Covenanters were strong in the south-west of Scotland, and especially in the hill country. They had charismatic leaders such as Alexander Peden, and while they never seriously threatened to topple the government, they were never roundly defeated either.

Religion and politics though, had another twist. Charles II had no legitimate children, and his heir, James II (and VII of Scotland) was an avowed Roman Catholic, who wished to restore that religion as the established religion of his kingdoms. James was also autocratic, and a revolution, orchestrated at a high level, removed James from the throne, sent the Stuarts into an exile from which they would twice attempt to return, settled William of Orange on the united thrones, and settled the matter of

church government in Scotland in favour of the Presbyterians. Not everyone was happy, especially the Catholics of Ireland but the upheaval of 1690 brought to an end a long period of unrest.

THE COVENANTER MARTYRS MEMORIAL 2005
A86711k (Rob Close)

Ayr, like many places in south-west Scotland, has its Covenanter martyrs. Their memorial in the kirkyard has been restored on many occasions.

William Adair became a minister in Ayr in 1639, and was a zealous supporter of the cause of Presbyterian worship. At his behest the Ayr Kirk Session had given thanks for the defeat of Charles at Marston Moor in 1644. A former soldier, Adair spent two years as a chaplain with the Scots army in Ireland and returned to Ayr in 1646. He was deeply involved in the tumult of the period, but was still minister when the new church - the Auld Kirk - was opened. In 1660 he was restricted to preaching in Ayr, but seems, perhaps mellowing with old age, to have worked alongside episcopally-minded men appointed as his curates. However, he was finally suspended from his post in 1681 and deposed in 1682, when he would no longer conform to the new Episcopal ways. He had been in post for 43 years, and had served as Ayr's minister for some of the most turbulent years the church had ever known.

THE STATUE OF WILLIAM ADAIR 2005
A86712k (Rob Close)

The Harbour

The town's merchants were dependent on the harbour if the town was to thrive; as late as 1808 a meeting of ship-owners in the town declared without the trade of the harbour Ayr 'would soon become a deserted village.' Ships were becoming bigger and bigger, and the tidal nature of Ayr's harbour was presenting difficulties. There was a sand bar across the mouth of the river on which, at low tides, ships could run aground. Travellers found Ayr's harbour worthy of comment. In 1578 it was 'a pretty sea port where strange nations often arrive and land, the port is so commodious', and in the 1590s work included the building of a quay. In the years after this, imports included wine, salt, foodstuffs (oranges being specifically mentioned), timber and animal hides, and we have already seen that this period saw Ayr's first ventures into the trans-Atlantic trade. In 1656, another traveller found that Ayr was 'growing every day worse and worse, by reason of the harbour being clogged and filled up with sand.' However these problems were overcome and the port continued to be Ayr's lifeblood. Even during the height of religious controversy, in June 1684 Ayr's town council organised a Glasgow engineer to come and sort out a wreck which had been blocking the entrance to the harbour since early the previous winter.

On the north side of the river, Newton-upon-Ayr was growing. Newton shared with Ayr access to the river. For many traders it had the advantages of being outside the control and influence of the town council and the leading burgess families that controlled Ayr's destiny. Wharves and shipyards developed on the Newton shore, and stoked the prosperity of the little burgh. A council house, or tollbooth, was built in Newton about 1647, and a market cross was put up in 1675.

NEWTON CROSS 2005 A86713k (Rob Close)

The Newton Cross has the inscription 'Neutoun 1675 Rebuilt 1775'. It was probably first erected close to the modern day junction of Main Street and King Street. It disappeared from view during the 19th century, but was found in a garden in Main Street and re-erected in its present position in 1905.

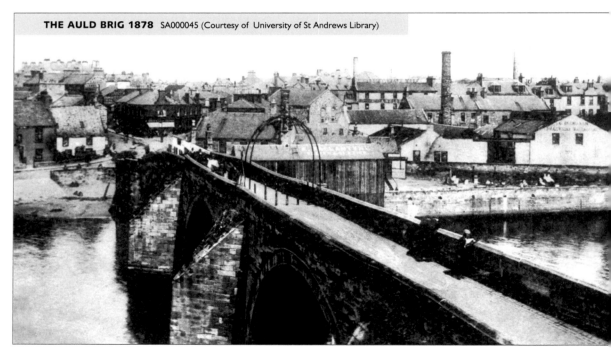

THE AULD BRIG 1878 SA000045 (Courtesy of University of St Andrews Library)

The industrial nature of Newton and Wallacetown is well seen in this 1878 photograph. On the left is the Black Bull, one of Ayr's oldest pubs, and still in business today.

In 1678 John Slezer, one of the King's Engineers, was in Ayr, and has left us the two earliest views we have of the town of Ayr. In the one we see here (ZZZ04152), the town is shown from a site on the Sandy Knowes, perhaps near where the Riverside Place high flats are. We can recognise the Auld Brig and the Auld Kirk, then a very new kirk indeed. In the middle of the skyline is the top of the Tolbooth, which was erected in 1575. The other view (reproduced in John Strawhorn's 'The History of Ayr') was taken from nearer the sea, but still on the north side, on the Newton Green. Again we can recognise the Auld Brig, and the Tolbooth is prominent. The old church, St John's Tower, and the buildings of Cromwell's fort can be seen. The harbour is busy with shipping, and a party of horsemen are galloping along the Newton shore.

Shortly before Slezer's visit, the town council of Ayr had acquired in 1673 the 'Auld Tower' in the High Street, which they raised by two storeys in 1731 to provide the people of the upper part of the town with a belfry and clock. By 1774 this building was known as the Wallace Tower.

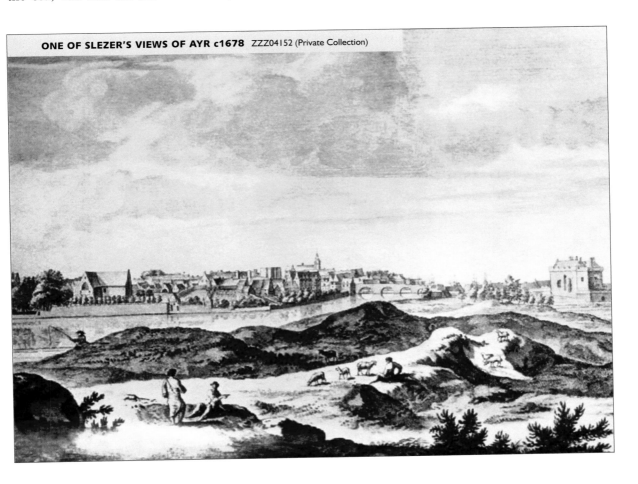

ONE OF SLEZER'S VIEWS OF AYR c1678 ZZZ04152 (Private Collection)

An Ayr Chevalier

Michael Ramsay rose from humble beginnings in Ayr to be one of the greatest religious scholars in France. Ramsay was born in 1686, near the Fish Cross. His father was a baker, and ambitious, and his son became a student at Edinburgh. Here he became attached to the Jacobite cause. Ramsay moved to Holland, to study at Leyden, and became a Roman Catholic, a move which led to estrangement from his family, and exile from Scotland. He moved to France, and from 1724-1726 was personal tutor to Charles Edward Stuart, the Young Pretender. After this he was offered the post of tutor to the young Duke of Cumberland, son of George II, but, because of his Jacobite sympathies, declined. Cumberland, of course, went on to defeat Charles Stewart on the battlefield of Culloden in 1746. Ramsay's final years were spent between Oxford and France, where he died in 1743. He was buried at St-Germain-en-Laye, near Paris. In the late 20th century St-Germain-en-Laye became Ayr's twin town.

Ayr was relatively untouched by the Jacobite uprisings of the Stuarts - James, the Old Pretender, in 1715, and his son, Charles Edward, the Young Pretender, in 1745 - although local militias were raised in case of trouble. Ayr was unlikely to find much common cause with the Stuarts and their advocacy of a return to a Catholic state. Instead it embraced the Hanoverian kings, as in 1714, when the accession of George II was celebrated in Ayr by bell-ringing, bonfires and volleys of gunfire in the town centre.

AYR 1900 46000x

This photograph of 1900 shows the congested nature of the medieval town.

CHAPTER THREE

Widening Horizons

BELLEISLE HOUSE HOTEL 1937 SA000047 (Courtesy of University of St Andrews Library)

IN 1754 THE TOWN COUNCIL of Ayr took the decision to sell the lands they owned at Alloway. These lands had been gifted to the town by the charter of 1205, and provided a steady stream of income. Now, however, the town council was in financial trouble. The accounts of 1753 showed that the town had earned £6,000, and was carrying a debt of around £8,200. Almost all the income was taken up on necessary expenses, and servicing this debt. The councillors also knew that a number of big funding projects could be no longer delayed: the bridge was in a dangerous condition, the tolbooth needed rebuilding, and if the harbour was not modernised soon, trade would decline. Selling Alloway may have been selling the family silver, but it offered a quick fix to a deepening problem.

The sale came at a good time. Ayr, with its balmy climate and mild winters, wa

Belleisle

Belleisle was first built around 1775 for Hugh Hamilton, who had made his fortune in the West Indies. The house was considerably enlarged in the 1830s for a descendent, Alexander West Hamilton. It was again enlarged around 1900, this time for George Coats, who had made his money from the cotton thread mills in Paisley. It was Coats who commissioned James Davidson to produce the remarkable woodcarvings in the house, illustrating the poems of Robert Burns. The house and grounds were acquired by the town council in 1926. The house was converted into a hotel, and it is still one of the best-known hotels in the town, while the fine gardens, still maintained by South Ayrshire Council, add to its charms and add lustre to its popularity as a setting for local weddings. The parkland was converted into two 18-hole golf courses, which further enhance its reputation.

BELLEISLE HOUSE HOTEL, THE FIREPLACE 1937 SA000065
(Courtesy of University of St Andrews Library)

becoming a place that was considered healthy, and a good place to retire to. It became popular with people who had made money both in the Americas and West Indies. Ayr also attracted Scots whose fortune came from further afield, and particularly India where, for those who survived the climate and the hazards of military life, service with either the forces of the British army or the administration of the East India Company was a sure way to a sizeable fortune. These people had money and wished to purchase small estates. The lands of Alloway offered them that opportunity, and a number of small estates were created. Two of these, Belleisle and Rozelle, played and continue to play a big part in Ayr's history.

The middle years of the 18th century saw Ayr, and Ayrshire, heavily involved in smuggling. The goods smuggled were those

BELLEISLE HOUSE HOTEL, THE GARDENS 1937
SA000062 (Courtesy of University of St Andrews Library)

BELLEISLE HOUSE HOTEL 1937 SA000047
(Courtesy of University of St Andrews Library)

BELLEISLE HOUSE HOTEL, THE ENTRANCE HALL 1937 SA000064 (Courtesy of University of St Andrews Library)

BELLEISLE HOUSE HOTEL, THE LILY POND 1937
SA000063 (Courtesy of University of St Andrews Library)

BELLEISLE HOUSE HOTEL, THE LILY POND 1937 SA000063 (Courtesy of University of St Andrews Library)

on which the highest duties were levied: wine and spirit, tobacco, sugar and salt. The long, dark Ayrshire coast made it a natural habitat for smuggling gangs, and it was also an easy sail from the Isle of Man, which lay outside British customs jurisdiction. Goods could be brought there legally and openly, and then shipped on, clandestinely, to small harbours and creeks on the coast, and then taken inland for sale in Glasgow and elsewhere. Many companies which had a legal aspect to their trade were also involved in the clandestine trade. Smuggling declined towards the end of the 18th century, particularly after the Isle of Man loophole was closed in 1765, and smuggling vessels were forced to make longer, and consequently more risky, voyages.

Did you know?
Washerwoman's Son Makes Good

James Macrae was the son of a poor washerwoman in Ayr. To seek his fortune he sailed to India, where he encountered good luck, and rose steadily to become the Governor of Madras. Returning to Britain, he first bought an estate in Kent, but came to Ayr in 1733. He found most of his relatives were dead, except a cousin, Hugh McGuire, who was a well-known fiddler, and a carpenter by trade. Macrae used his fortune to set up Hugh McGuire and his daughters in estates in different parts of Scotland, and two of the fiddler's daughters became Lady Glencairn and Lady Barjarg. Macrae bought the estate of Monkton for himself; he renamed it Orangefield because of his support for William III, and also paid for the statue of William which still stands outside Glasgow Cathedral. The monument he built for himself still stands near Monkton and can be seen close to the Monkton Lodge roundabout.

Alexander Oliphant & Co

One of the leading smuggling concerns was Alexander Oliphant & Co, an Ayr firm of wine merchants, founded in 1766. Many of the people involved in this company were from the Isle of Man, or had strong connections there, while Oliphant himself had been an employee of the Excise. The company also had an 'above-board' shipping business, which still flourishes, though it has changed hands several times. The company's offices in Academy Street have impressive cellars under the houses capable of holding immeasurable amounts of wine.

Rozelle

Rozelle was built soon after 1754 for Robert Hamilton, uncle of Hugh Hamilton who built Belleisle. It is named after his estate in Jamaica. It was enlarged, with wings to either side around 1830. The house remained with the Hamilton family until 1968, when it was gifted to the town council by the family. Today, Rozelle is a thriving museum and art gallery, with changing exhibitions and attractive shop and tea-room. The art collection has a strong modern feel, and includes a Henry Moore reclining nude, and a series of granite sculptures by Ronald Rae in the landscaped grounds behind the house. The grounds are now largely devoted to well-used sports pitches and woodland walks. Every year the popular Holy Fair, a major opportunity for local charities to raise funds and awareness, is held in the grounds of Rozelle.

ROZELLE 2005 A86714k (Rob Close)

Robert Burns

Robert Burns was born in Alloway on 25 January 1759. His father, William, was a gardener who had come to Ayrshire from the north-east of Scotland. Robert was educated in Alloway by a well-respected Ayr teacher called William Murdoch. He was also sent to his mother's relatives in Kirkoswald for a time, to be educated at the parish school there. Burns was a restless character, and tried a number of career options before settling on farming. The family took a lease of Lochlea farm, near Tarbolton, and it was here, and subsequently at Mossgiel near Mauchline, that Burns grew up, and wrote his first, brilliant, poetry. Farming was hard, and Robert was on the verge of emigrating to the West Indies, when, almost as a farewell gesture, he arranged to have his 'Poems, Chiefly in the Scottish Dialect', published by John Wilson in Kilmarnock in 1790. The book was an immediate success, and thoughts of emigration were abandoned as he was feted by the great and the good of Edinburgh. More poetry followed, but the splendour and pomp of Edinburgh paled, and the countryman in Burns reasserted itself. He returned to Ayrshire, to Mauchline, with his devoted, if occasionally sorely tried wife, Jean Armour. But Burns failed to settle, and they moved next to Ellisland Farm, near Dumfries, where he tried, unsuccessfully, to make a go of life as a farmer. At Ellisland he wrote his last great poem, 'Tam o' Shanter'. This he did in the course of a single walk along the banks of the river Nith, and without paper, producing a poem that required but little amendment. From Ellisland the family moved into Dumfries, where Robert got a job with the Excise Service. However, his health, which had never been robust, failed him, and he died on 21 July 1796, the end perhaps hastened by the sea-bathing cure recommended by his doctors. Burns's lasting fame rests not only on his poetry, but also his letters, his collecting and recording of folk songs (a field in which he was considerably ahead of his time), and the joyous, carefree swagger with which he approached life.

PORTRAIT OF ROBERT BURNS 1897 39858b

BURNS'S COTTAGE 1897 39858

BURNS'S COTTAGE, ALLOWAY 1887 SA000070
(Courtesy of University of St Andrews Library)

BURNS'S COTTAGE, ALLOWAY, THE INTERIOR 1887
SA000042 (Courtesy of University of St Andrews Library)

BURNS'S COTTAGE, ALLOWAY 1878 SA000046 (Courtesy of University of St Andrews Library)

Our photographs show Burns's Cottage when it was still a public house in the closing years of the 19th century.

CUTTY SARK ZZZ04153 (Private Collection)

This print shows the witch in the short skirt (the 'cutty' sark) who pursued Tam o' Shanter from Alloway Old Kirk to the Brig o' Doon.

The sale of the Alloway lands was a success. The sum raised was more than the councillors had expected, and laid the basis for a community fund - the Common Good Fund - that has continued to assist local organisations and individuals to this day. Although faced with many calls on their funds, the council did not move rashly. First, they turned their attention to the harbour, and in 1772 control of the port passed to the Ayr Harbour Trustees, a body with representatives

from both the council and the merchant and ship-owners using the harbour. Small improvements were made, but the trustees were reluctant to commit money (especially their money) to the wholesale change that was required. Reports were commissioned from a raft of notable engineers, such as Watt, Smeaton and Rennie, read, approved and quietly forgotten.

In 1772 Ayr suffered a major financial calamity. The Ayr Bank, which had been formed by John Macadam & Co in 1763, had been taken over by Douglas, Heron & Co in 1768. This company, which was backed

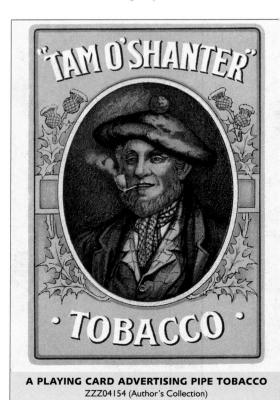

A PLAYING CARD ADVERTISING PIPE TOBACCO
ZZZ04154 (Author's Collection)

Burns's characters have always provided popular brand names.

by many of the landowners and wealthy merchants of the south-west of Scotland, lent imprudently, and often to its directors, shareholders and close family. It was over-stretched, and when a London bank on which it had relied failed in 1772, Douglas, Heron & Co had no choice but to follow suit. Payments were suspended on 12 June 1772, and the Bank closed, permanently, on 12 August 1773, leaving behind a massive debt, and a tangle of loans and securities. The shareholders were responsible for the debts, which amounted to £700,000 (a staggering sum in today's terms), and the responsibility bankrupted and ruined many of them, forcing estates to be sold, businesses to be sold, and generally delaying throughout the south-west the increasing agricultural and industrial change that was beginning to spread through the country. It was not until 1804 that the affairs of Douglas, Heron & Co were formally wound up.

LONGHILL AVENUE 1900 46004

Longhill Avenue was a popular destination for a walk from Ayr. The trees were taken down in 1962.

However, improvement was in the air. The first priority for the council was a new bridge. The Old Bridge was narrow, inconvenient and in need of major repairs. A new bridge, it was argued, would be wider, would create a better approach to the town from the north and, in the modern style, would be more sympathetic to Georgian taste than the old bridge. The council went immediately to the best architect of the day, Robert Adam, and asked him to design a bridge. He did, but the council, prudent as ever, felt unable to meet the costs of this bridge, and asked another architect, Alexander Stevens, to design a similar but cheaper one. Stevens did so, and his bridge was opened with much pomp and ceremony in November 1788. This first New

Bridge, perhaps because economies had been made when it was built, became unsafe and was demolished in 1877-1878, to be replaced by the present New Bridge.

The opening of the New Bridge meant that traffic now came into Ayr along what was known as the Water Vennel (today's New Bridge Street), and was immediately confronted by the Tolbooth and the Malt Cross. The Malt Cross was removed almost as soon as the bridge was open and in use, but the Tolbooth remained an impediment to traffic for another 40 years or so. It was declared unsafe in the early 1800s but lingered on as an increasingly rickety and insecure prison until 1822, when the final 21 prisoners were transferred to the new gaol in the county

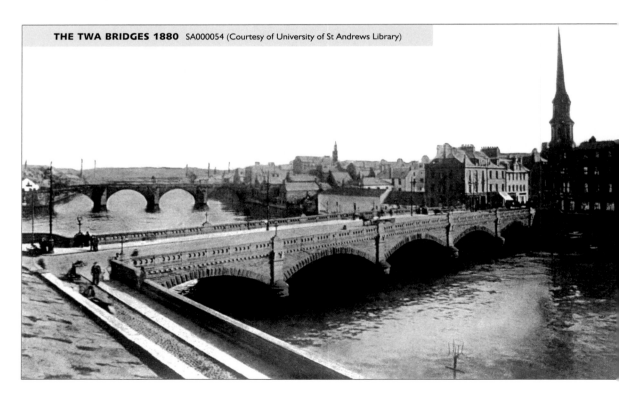

THE TWA BRIDGES 1880 SA000054 (Courtesy of University of St Andrews Library)

buildings, and it was demolished in 1826, giving a better approach to the town and improving the character of Sandgate.

Municipal aspiration was not lacking on the north side of the river either. The town of Newton began to grow noticeably in the 18th century, as did the neighbouring settlement of Wallacetown, in the parish of St Quivox. Here were to be found the workshops, the small industries, the poor and the transient who were unable to live and work in Ayr. Perhaps a little rough at the edges, this was a vibrant place with its own civic pride. Newton's wealth was based on two main industries - coal mining and shipbuilding. Both these industries benefited not only the people, and brought them into the area to work, but also were of direct benefit to the town itself. The Newton town council had an interest in the lands of the freemen, where the coal was found, and in the ownership of the north bank of the river, where the shipyards were. To mark their wealth and their civic pride, in the late 18th century they built a new church, now demolished, to make way for the King Street dual carriageway, and a new town house. The town house was completed in 1788, though much of it was also demolished to make way for the dual carriageway. The remainder, known as the Newton Steeple, stands proudly, if in isolation, as a reminder that Newton, too, has a long and honourable history.

THE TWA BRIDGES 1937 SA000041 (Courtesy of University of St Andrews Library)

These pictures of the second New Bridge, taken nearly 60 years apart, show many changes in transport, while Ayr's trams had come and gone in the intervening period.

NEWTON STEEPLE ZZZ04155 (Private Collection)

The first Tolbooth in Newton was recorded in about 1647. It probably survived until it was replaced by this structure in 1795 which originally had extensions to either side which housed the offices of the freemen of Newton. These were demolished in the 1960s, to make way for new roads, leaving the steeple to stand alone as a symbol of Newton and its independent spirit. Roderick Lawson, a late 19th-century minister of Maybole, asked: 'Did the bailies design thee at a public dinner, and was thy model taken from a square gin bottle with an inverted glass on top, or was it an old-fashioned penny-loaf surmounted by an extinguisher?'

As we have seen, the last years of the 18th century saw the reconstruction of the Ayr Academy. The town was growing. Not only was a bigger school needed, but there was also a need for more church space. The Auld Kirk was crowded, and in 1810 a second established church - known as the New Church - was opened in Fort Street, alongside the new Academy. Designed by a well-known Glasgow architect, David Hamilton, this was in a classical style, and marked another step on Ayr's transformation from a medieval to a modern town.

Until the late 18th century most people, of all classes, had lived in the main streets of the town, their houses intermingled with their business premises all along the length of the High Street and Sandgate, and in the lesser streets such as Carrick Street and Newmarket Street, which had been begun in 1767. Now, however, those who could afford to wished to live in more salubrious conditions, with space, privacy and the benefits of a garden. They began to build, and move to, the Georgian terraces which characterise the southern edge of the town centre, in streets such as Barns Street, Charlotte Street and, most impressively, Wellington Square. These houses were popular with wealthy local businessmen, especially solicitors and doctors, with the local landed families, and with Scots who had worked abroad and had come back to Scotland to retire. Barns Street was nicknamed Maidens Row for many years, due to the number of unmarried women, often daughters of the landed families, who owned property there.

John Loudon MacAdam

SANDGATE, LADY CATHCART'S HOUSE 2005
A86716k (Rob Close)

JOHN LOUDON MACADAM MONUMENT
2005   A86717k (Rob Close)

One of the oldest houses in Ayr, in Sandgate, is known as Lady Cathcart's House. It is believed that in this house, in 1756, John Loudon MacAdam, the world famous road surveyor, was born. As a successful New York businessman MacAdam made a fortune, and also married well. He returned to Ayrshire in 1783. He bought an estate - Sauchrie - near Maybole, where he is said to have carried out his first experiments in road construction. Financial problems led him to leave Scotland, and to pursue a career as a road surveyor in England, before returning to Scotland, where he died at Moffat in 1836. MacAdam's advance was to recognise the greater stability of graded road surfaces, with layers of increasingly smaller stones - a macadamised road. Despite being a partner in the Earl of Dundonald's tar works at Muirkirk, he failed to recognise the extra stability that a binding, such as tar, would bring to his techniques. It was another century or so before other minds saw the possibility, and began to roll out 'tar-macadamised' (or tarmac) roads. John Loudon MacAdam is commemorated in Ayr by a monument in Wellington Square.

Wellington Square saw the next big expression of civic pride, when the county buildings were opened in 1822. This fine classical structure, which dominates the square from its position at the west end, was designed to hold both the administration of the county council (formally known as the Commissioners of Supply) and of the local sheriff court. Behind the main building there was also the new gaol. The building has been extended on a couple of occasions, and the gaol has been demolished, but it still serves as offices for the local authority (South Ayrshire Council), and the sheriff court, and regular sittings of the high court of justiciary, are still held here.

Robert Burns remained a national hero. His place of birth was becoming a place of pilgrimage, even though the family cottage was now a public house. Something a little more dignified was required, and it was agreed that a monument should be erected. The Edinburgh architect Thomas Hamilton was selected (and he volunteered to work for free, a decision which did him no harm, as we shall see), and designed the Greek style monument that we see today. The monument was begun in 1820, and formally opened in 1823. In the elegant grounds there are statues of Tam o' Shanter and Souter Johnny, crafted by the self-taught sculptor, James Thom.

WELLINGTON SQUARE 1939 SA000515
(Courtesy of University of St Andrews Library)

Wellington Square is shown here with formal gardens and war memorial, and with the County Buildings and the Pavilion in the distance. The County Buildings and Court House were completed in 1822.

A Duel

The foundation stone of the Burns's Monument was laid by Sir Alexander Boswell, son of James Boswell, the famous diarist and biographer, and a man of considerable ability, best known for the printing press he established at his home, Auchinleck House. In 1822, however, he was called out in a duel by a political opponent. In the duel, which took place near another Boswell estate in Fife to avoid the authorities in Edinburgh, Sir Alexander was wounded and died the following day. His opponent fled to France. This was one of the last high-profile fatal duels in Britain. Sir Alexander was not, therefore, able to perform the opening ceremony in 1824.

BURNS'S MONUMENT 1897 39862

The Burns's Monument at Alloway in its garden setting.

BURNS'S MONUMENT AND THE SHELL GROTTO 1900 46007

TAM O' SHANTER AND SOUTER JOHNNY 1897 39859

James Thom's statues of Tam o' Shanter and Souter Johnnie. Thom also sculpted the William Wallace statue on the Wallace Tower.

Thomas Hamilton's reward for his gesture over his fees for the Burns's Monument came swiftly. In 1828 the town council, perhaps smarting at the grandeur of the county's new buildings, began to build a new town's buildings, on the corner of New Bridge Street and High Street. Thomas Hamilton was the architect chosen, and in the crowning spire, which soars to 225 feet, he has given the town a powerful icon, and the finest town spire anywhere in Scotland.

The Town's Buildings

Thomas Hamilton's town's buildings occupy the New Bridge Street frontage. The complex was greatly enlarged around 1881 when a new town hall, with various offices, was erected behind, with a main façade to the High Street. The whole was badly damaged by fire in 1897, and most of the interior, including the existing town hall, was rebuilt after that, by the Ayr architect James Kennedy Hunter. The building remains in use for local authority administration, and some minor court work. The hall remains a popular and well-used venue for concerts and other events, and concerts from here are regularly broadcast on BBC Radio 3.

SANDGATE STREET 1900 46003

Oscar Wilde

In December 1883 Oscar Wilde delivered a lecture in Ayr town hall on 'The House Beautfiul'. At that time Wilde was at the height of his fame, and had been parodied by Gilbert and Sullivan, and his presence in Ayr generated an extraordinary demand for tickets, while the local press commented in great detail on his clothes, noting that the only conspicuous display of colour was a pink silk handkerchief. His talk, which was humorous and well received, echoed the then popular desire to move away from the heavy and over-full decoration which we associate with the Victorians.

> ## *Did you know?*
>
> *In August 1919 the spire of the Town's Buildings was climbed by a young typist, Annie Hutton.*

With civic pride and civic achievement came a greater sense of tolerance. Roman Catholics were no longer seen as a threat to the stability of the nation. They had been allowed to worship freely. Largely as a result of Irish emigration into the industrial suburbs of Ayr, there was a substantial, and growing, Catholic community in Ayr by the 1820s, and in 1827 their church of St Margaret's, in John Street on the north side of the river, was opened and still remains as one of their main centres of worship in the town.

Thomas Hamilton was back in Ayr again in the 1830s when he was asked to replace the old Wallace Tower, which stood in the High Street close to the entrance to the town from the north and east. It is not proven that the old tower, whose name seems to be a corruption of 'wall-house', had any connection with William Wallace, but local legend says that it is so, and is not to be gainsaid. Hamilton's castellated Gothic tower marks the old building line, and now juts out into the High Street, left behind when this part of the High Street was largely rebuilt in the 1870s and 1880s. The Wallace Tower was begun in 1830 but, due to 'an unfortunate accident', had to be taken down and rebuilt in 1833, and was completed finally in 1834. A niche in one wall contains a statue, by James Thom, of William Wallace.

> ## *Did you know?*
>
> *It is said that two men from Maybole, coming into Ayr on the day that the statue of Wallace was being hoisted into position, saw this happening. They assumed that it was the preparations for a hanging and, being fearful of this novel form of execution, fled hotfoot back to Maybole.*

The Wallace Tower is seen as it was in 1900. James Ritchie moved his drapers business here in 1887, and it remained a drapery store until 1962. Robert Hyslop who owned it for the final 40 years began in 1908 as an apprentice on 2s 6d (12½p) a week. In the 1920s a pair of blankets cost £1 10s (£1.50) and an embroidered tea cloth 4s 11d (24½p).

An Ayr Radical

In the cemetery at Wallacetown there is a statue, erected in 1859, of Dr John Taylor (1805-1842). John Taylor was a member of the family that owned the Blackhouse estate and who were among the major coal owners in the area. John Taylor, as a young man, was taken up with the cause of radical politics, and became a firebrand politician. He travelled throughout Britain campaigning for an extension of the franchise and as a supporter of the People's Charter, and was considered one of the most dangerous Chartists by the Government. However, Taylor's health broke and he left politics. He died near Larne, in Northern Ireland, where his brother-in-law was a minister in the Church of Ireland.

THE STATUE OF JOHN TAYLOR, WALLACETOWN 2005 A86718k (Rob Close)

AYR FROM THE AIR 1972 AFA222852

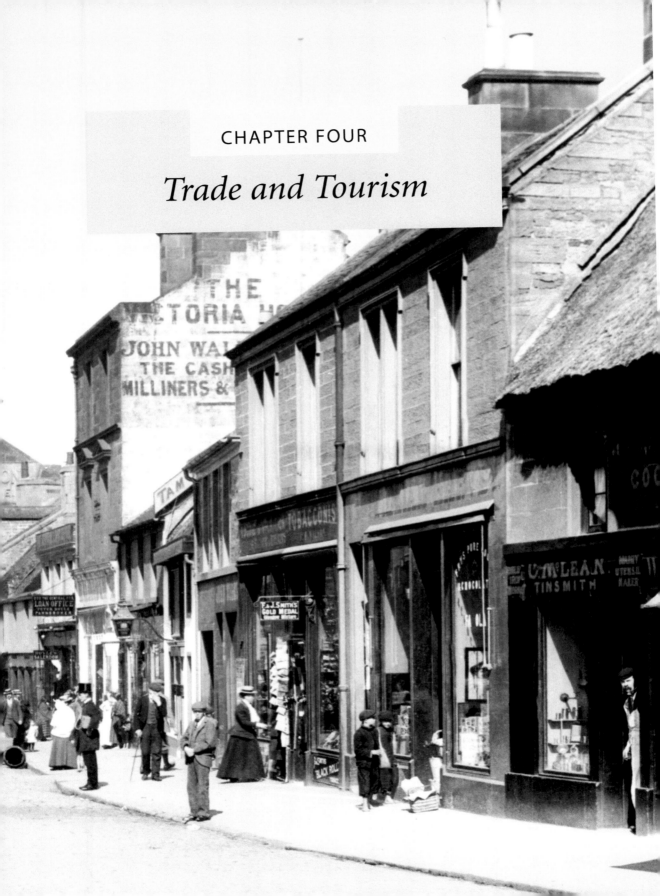

CHAPTER FOUR

Trade and Tourism

IN 1837 WILLIAM IV, the sailor king, died, to be succeeded on the throne by his young niece, Victoria. Two years later, in 1839, the first railway station in Ayr was opened. A new chapter in the life of Britain, and of Ayr, was beginning.

Railed transport was not a new phenomenon for the people of Ayr and Newton. Waggonways, using horses to draw rakes of waggons, had existed since the late 18th century. They were used to bring coal from the pits in Newton, and further inland towards Whitletts and Auchincruive to the harbour at Ayr, where the coal was loaded into ships for export to Ireland. There was also a longer waggonway linking the pits in and around Kilmarnock with the sea at Troon, to the north of Ayr. This was initially worked with horses, but a steam engine had been introduced experimentally in the early 19th century. This waggonway, although used mostly for goods transport, also had the facilities to convey passengers.

The major breakthrough came with the development of reliable steam propulsion, and the realisation that railways could be used for passenger transport. The success of early lines such as the Stockton and Darlington, and the Liverpool and Manchester, demonstrated that there was an untapped market for rail travel and the rail boom took off. It was natural that an early proposal was for a line between Ayr and Glasgow; there was already a regular traffic between the two towns, both by sea and by road, over the bleak Fenwick Moor.

The Glasgow Paisley and Kilmarnock and Ayr Railway Company was formed in 1836. Archibald Hamilton of Rozelle was one of the original directors. The line obtained the necessary Parliamentary consent in July 1837, and two years later the first special train took the directors over the new line from Ayr to Irvine. The line opened between Ayr and Irvine in August 1839, and opened in stages until through running between Glasgow and Ayr began on 12 August 1840.

Did you know?
The Station

Ayr's first station was on the north side of the river, in North Harbour Street, and this remained the terminus until a new station was opened, where the present station stands, in 1857, as the railways expanded in all directions. The original station remained as a goods station until the 1950s. Our illustration shows the grand opening of the line through to Glasgow in 1840.

THE STATION 1840 ZZZ04156 (Private Collection)

Did you know?
The Eglinton Tournament

One of the grandest and most spectacular events staged in Victorian Britain was the Eglinton Tournament, held at Eglinton castle, near Irvine, in 1839. This fantasy recreation of a medieval tournament, with knights, ladies of honour, jousting, balls and much merriment, proved to be outstandingly popular with the locals of Ayrshire, who flocked to see it, and made great use of the newly opened railway to get themselves to Irvine, causing the young railway company to run many special and additional trains to cope with the demand.

Franz Liszt

An early traveller on the railway was the Hungarian composer Franz Liszt, who was travelling from Ireland to Glasgow as part of a concert tour in January 1841. His party was delayed by bad weather and arrived in Ayr by boat - the 'Sir William Wallace' - from Stranraer one morning. Liszt was due to give a concert in Glasgow that afternoon and, luckily, there was a special train leaving Ayr at 11 o'clock. This 'special' train consisted of open cattle trucks and open third class coaches, with plank seating, in which Liszt and his party travelled for three and a half hours to Glasgow, through a freezing landscape, in the company of cows and pigs to arrive in Glasgow, coal-black and half-dead, to discover the concert had been postponed.

The opening of the railway gave a further boost to Ayr's increasing popularity as a place for holidays, and as a place to live in. The view across the bay, with the romantic backdrop of the island of Arran, had been proclaimed to be as beautiful as that of the bay of Naples, while the mild climate, with balmy winters and pleasant warm summers, had led others to call Ayr the 'Montpellier of Scotland'. Certainly, it offered plenty of scope for sea-bathing, which was becoming increasingly fashionable, and was within a day's range of many 'must see' sights, such as Culzean Castle (the Robert Adam designed mansion of the Kennedy family, perched on the cliffs 15 miles south of Ayr), Ness Glen (where the River Doon flows through a deep, narrow gorge) and Ballochmyle Viaduct (near Mauchline, and opened in 1848, which was then, and is still, the largest single-span stone bridge in the world), but particularly, as always, the shrines of Burns.

For those who chose to settle in Ayr, there was a busy social scene, led by the county families from their homes in Wellington Square, but there were regular balls and concerts, and many other entertainments.

THE TAM O' SHANTER INN 1900 46005

The Tam o' Shanter Inn in 1900. The lady waiting watchfully at the door is Christina Scott, the landlord's wife.
Her husband John was mine host here from 1883 until his death in 1906.

The Theatre that became a Church

Usually churches are adapted to other uses, but in Ayr a theatre became a church. The Theatre Royal, in Fort Street, was opened in 1815, though it was known for most of its existence as the Queen's Rooms. In 1878 it was sold by the owners to the Baptist congregation in Ayr, who converted the building into a church, and it still operates as a church today, and was thoroughly restored in 2004. In Ayr, churches have also been adapted for other uses: two are now theatres, one is a dance studio and one is a popular pub in the Sandgate.

THE OLD THEATRE ROYAL 2005 A86719k (Rob Close)

The first years of Victoria's reign were marked by division within the Church of Scotland, and the formation, in 1843, of the Free Church of Scotland, which joined the United Presbyterians as the leading voices of dissension. The result was a growth in the number of churches, which was also coupled with a big expansion in the population of Ayr through the latter half of the century. As a result many of Ayr's churches date from the second half of the 19th century. Of these perhaps the grandest is St Andrew's in Park Circus, built in 1893 for the Free Church of Scotland. This congregation had only come into being in 1889, as a result of a dispute within the Wallacetown Free Church, and was sanctioned by the church only on the condition that they built in an area of the town that was then growing. As a result, the congregation moved from one of the poorer parts of Ayr to an area that was new and wealthy. The minister, William Hay, was determined to have a proper church, and

THE COSINA CORSET ZZZ04157 (Private Collection)

John McCulloch, 'fancy draper and corset specialist' ran his shop at 171-173 High Street from 1912 to 1929. The business was continued by his son until 1958, when their premises became the Provincial Building Society. This model, Model I, cost 3s 11d (19½p).

after some brisk fund-raising, this fine red sandstone building was completed.

Other notable churches from this period of growth include St Leonard's in St Leonard's Road, St Columba in Midton Road, and St James's in North Newton, whose smoke-blackened tower is a particular landmark near Newton-on-Ayr station.

Schools, too, increased in number through the 19th century. Their growth was boosted by the Education Act of 1872 which introduced the concept of universal education, and the first steps towards a free education system. One school which dates from this period is Holmston Primary School, which began life as Smith's Institution.

HOARDINGS AT ALLOWAY STREET AND DALBLAIR ROAD JUNCTION 1897 39864x

The hoardings on this vacant site at the junction of Alloway Street and Dalblair Road carry adverts for well-known Ayr businesses such as the photographer Ambrose Bara, the confectioner Louis le Clair and the popular Hotel Dalblair.

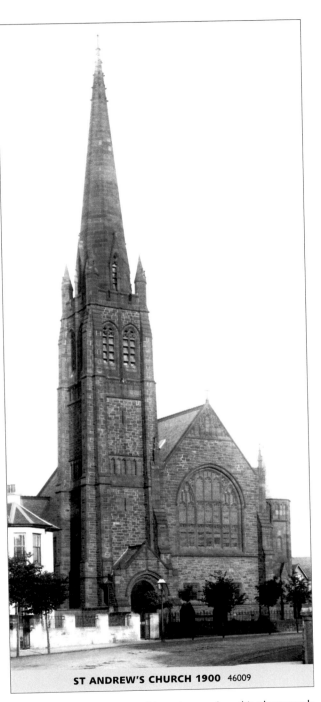

ST ANDREW'S CHURCH 1900 46009

St Andrew's Church was still brand new when this photograph was taken in 1900.

Smith's Institution

John Smith was a sea captain in Ayr who bequeathed his fortune to found a school where the children of the poor could be educated free of charge. Smith's school began in 1825, in a room in the poor house, and gradually expanded until the present school in Holmston Road was built in 1884, by which time Smith's Institution, which was administered by the town, had been absorbed into the schooling system of the burgh. However 'it surely betokens a generous and enlightened spirit in days when the lot of the labouring classes was hard that Smith should have thought the education of the poor worth spending his fortune upon and a thing of which even paupers' children were worthy', and it is sad that he is not still commemorated in the name of the school.

HIGH STREET 1900 46002

Pedestrians and horses dominate the busy High Street in 1900.

Another school which has its roots in the 19th century is Wellington School. This independent school, originally for girls, was established in Wellington Square in the late 19th century, but may have connections with an earlier girls school in the square. This was in existence by 1850, and was run by Helen McClure, the Ayr-born wife of Solomon Gross, a native of Switzerland who taught French at Ayr Academy. Today, Wellington School is one of Scotland's leading independent schools, offering education at all levels to girls and boys.

The Victorian age also saw improvements in the provision of services for the sick and the poor. The first homes for the poor had been humble and unpretentious buildings, but in 1860 a new poor house was opened in Holmston Road, where the poor (and especially those who were too sick or too old to work) could be looked after. Today it is known as Holmston House, and is a major centre for social work in Ayr. It is a very attractive and well maintained building in a neo-Jacobean style. The author of a guide to Ayr published in 1870 noted that 'the first object that attracts the attention is a fine palace-like building ... and it has surprised not a few on being told that this is the Poor-House ... It has accommodation for 168 inmates, but since its erection the average number has been about 100. It cost somewhere about £10,000 and the ratepayers have for the last ten years felt, and will continue for a long time to feel, that a much less pretentious and costly building might have sufficiently well served the purpose for

ARCHIBALD GUTHRIE PREMISES
ZZZ04158 (Private Collection)

Archibald Guthrie, hosier and wool merchant, ran a successful business in the Winton Buildings for 30 years until he retired in 1896. The business was continued by John Macarthur, and survived until 1954, when the premises were absorbed by the expanding Clydesdale Bank.

which it was erected.' Perhaps, but foresight has given us a fine building which has served its purpose for nearly 150 years, and which is an ornament to the town.

The early hospitals in Ayr (and the first mention of a hospital in the town is in 1604) were also humble structures. A hospital for the mentally ill was built at Glengall in 1869. This has been known as the Ailsa Hospital since 1958. The original buildings still survive, though the hospital has been extended many times, and it has changed, as attitudes to psychiatric health have changed, but it too, like Holmston House, still serves the purpose for which it was built; another example of the wisdom and foresight of our Victorian forebears.

In 1883 a general hospital, known as Ayr County Hospital, was opened in Holmston Road, on a site close to Holmston House. In the days before the National Health Service, hospitals relied solely on donations and other charitable gifts, Ayr County Hospital being no exception. It provided an important service to the people of Ayr until 1992, when it was replaced by the new state-of-the-art Ayr Hospital, at Glengall, close to the Ailsa Hospital. There were also specialised hospitals at Heathfield (now a busy out-patient clinic) and Crofthead (now a caravan site) for infectious illnesses, a maternity hospital at Thornyflat and a children's hospital at Seafield. In 2004, to mark the 400th anniversary of hospital services in Ayr, a carved stone plaque from the Ayr County Hospital was re-erected at the new Ayr Hospital. It shows the Good Samaritan, a symbol of the charitable support on which the original hospital relied.

THE GOOD SAMARITAN PLAQUE 2005
A86720k (Rob Close)

The Good Samaritan at his new home at Ayr Hospital photographed in 2005.

Seafield

Before it became a hospital for children, Seafield House was the home of Sir William Arrol, who died in 1913. William Arrol was a self-taught engineer, who started his working life in the cotton mills of Paisley, and rose to be one of the world's greatest bridge builders. He is best known for the magnificent Forth Bridge, but also for the second Tay Rail Bridge, and for many other bridges throughout the world. Arrol moved to Seafield in 1888, and spent the rest of his life in Ayr. Scotland has given many great engineers to the world; Arrol is perhaps one of the greatest.

A cotton mill had been established in Charlotte Street just before 1800. In 1832 this mill was taken over by James Templeton who reconstructed it as a carpet factory. The business did well, and Templetons made not only their own carpets but also provided yarn for other carpet manufacturers throughout the United Kingdom. In the late 1860s the factory employed over 500, including 150 weavers making carpets. The mill was the site, on 16 June 1876, of Ayr's biggest tragedy of modern times. The mill caught fire, and 29 people (28 of them women) were killed. Templetons built a new mill in Mill Street, where they concentrated on making carpet and knitting yarns. This mill closed and was demolished in 1986.

THE AYR ARMS 1880 SA000516
(Courtesy of University of St Andrews Library)

The Ayr Arms was a long-established and well-known hostelry. It was known as Mattha' Dickie's. Matthew Dickie was the licensee for over 55 years, from 1899 to 1955.

The 19th century was the great period of industrial expansion. Ayr was never an industrial centre in the same way that its great rival, Kilmarnock, was. The growing tourist industry, and the business of local government and law enforcement, made major contributions to Ayr's wealth. Industry however was not neglected.

A 19TH-CENTURY BILL FROM THE AYR ARMS ZZZ04159
(Private Collection)

THE CEMETERY MONUMENT TO THOSE KILLED IN THE 1876 FIRE PHOTOGRAPHED IN 2005 A86721k (Rob Close)

Carpets were also made by William C Gray & Sons at their factory in McCall's Avenue. William Gray began his working life in Templetons mill, before establishing his own business in 1875. The company continued to make their 'Ayrtoun' carpets at the Newton Carpet Works until 1974.

Alexander Begg & Co Ltd still makes tweeds and cashmere at its mill in Viewfield Avenue. This business has its roots in the late 19th century. The mill was first built in 1882 for the making of machine lace, but after it was taken over by Beggs in 1902 it switched to the manufacture of tweed. The company continues to thrive, and the mill shop is a popular attraction for tourists and locals alike.

THREE DIFFERENT PLAYING CARD DESIGNS, ALL ADVERTISING GRAY'S CARPETS
ZZZ04160, ZZZ04161, ZZZ04162 (Author's Collection)

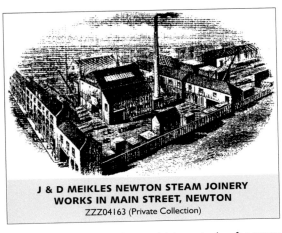

**J & D MEIKLES NEWTON STEAM JOINERY
WORKS IN MAIN STREET, NEWTON**
ZZZ04163 (Private Collection)

The Meikles were builders and joiners in Ayr for many years in the late 19th and early 20th centuries.

The Hawkhill Chemical Works of W G Walker & Sons was established in the early 1890s. William Walker, who had worked in the gas industry, and his sons had realised the potential of tar as a road material, shortly after the process and benefits of tarring a macadamised road had been accidentally discovered in Derbyshire. Walkers moved swiftly to establish themselves as one of the leading Scottish businesses in this field, and quickly obtained a country-wide reputation, which they retain to this day. The major engineering businesses were engaged in stamping and forging components, especially for ship building and mining. The Scottish Stamping and Engineering Co Ltd began in West Sanquhar Road in 1900, making 'ships' stanchions, cargo hooks, cleats and other ships' fittings', while James Dickie & Co made drop forgings at its Victoria Stamp Works from 1912.

The major industries of Ayr throughout the 19th century and into the 20th century remained the same as they had been in 1800:

coal mining, the harbour and shipbuilding. These three industries were obviously closely connected with each other.

Ayr is where it is because of the harbour. Originally ships had been berthed on the riverbanks on either side, which would have been exposed at low tide. During the middle ages wharves had been built, usually of wood, and some attempts had been made to build quays and breakwaters to improve the effectiveness of the harbour, and to increase the amount of shelter offered. By 1800 ships were increasing in size, and Ayr was beginning to suffer from the competition offered by newly built harbours such as Troon and Ardrossan. The Harbour Trustees

(who had been created in 1772 to look afte the harbour) responded by building ne stone wharves and quays on both sides of the river, with facilities for transhippin coal from waggons to boats. They bui breakwaters, and acquired a dredger, t ensure that the harbour was kept as deep a possible. They also improved navigation b building new lighthouses and beacons. I the late 19th century a further leap forwar was made, with the construction of dock which allowed shipping to be dealt with a all states of the tide. The large new wet doc on the Newton side of the river, was bui between 1874 and 1878, and was largel funded by James Baird of Cambusdoon.

THE PIER 1900 45999

The harbour mouth is seen here in 1900 with an elegant steam yacht offshore. From the 19th century sailing has been a popular activity on the Firth of Clyde, even if not all the yachts and dinghies to be seen on a sunny summer weekend are as grand as this one!

James Baird (1802-1876)

Baird was a member of the Lanarkshire-based family which in the 19th century made an immense fortune through its interests in coal and iron mining and manufacture. With his fortune, James Baird was able to buy a number of estates, including the one near Alloway on which he built himself a fine mansion, known as Cambusdoon. Gruff and plainly spoken, Baird was also deeply religious, and a generous benefactor of charities. In Ayr, however, he did not always endear himself to the people. He was at loggerheads with them over the siting of a new church in Alloway, which many feared would ruin the ambience of the Burns's shrines, and again over access to spring water from his estate for the town's water supply. His generous funding of the wet dock was perhaps due as much to a recognition of its value to his fellow mine-owners and industrialists as to a desire to benefit the town of Ayr.

Docks on the south side of the river were constructed for the shipbuilding industry. Until the second half of the 19th century most shipbuilding had been carried on in yards and on slips on the north side of the river. The new slip dock was built between 1880 and 1883. The first tenants of the dock and adjoining shed were McKnight McCreadie & Co, and their first new vessel was launched in September 1883. The yard was taken over in 1902 by the Ailsa Shipbuilding Co Ltd, who ran it until 1929, during which time they built and launched 144 vessels. During the Second World War, and for some years after, the yard was used for ship repair, but it was closed by 1971. The yards have now been demolished, and the slip dock acts as a feature of the post-millennial housing at the south harbour.

The Ayrshire coal industry continued to prosper during the Victorian period. Technological advances meant that coal could now be brought from further beneath

Did you know?
First and Last

The first boat to be launched from the Ayr shipyard was the 237-ton steam ship 'Elagh Hall' in 1883. The last was the 477-ton dredger 'Durdham' launched in 1929 for the Bristol Sand & Gravel Co, and sunk by a mine in the Bristol Channel in July 1940. The largest was the steam ship 'Drake', of 1,597 tons, launched in 1922 for the General Steam Navigation Co. The 'Drake' was sold to the Government of Zanzibar in 1934 and renamed 'Al Said'.

the ground. At the same time, the conditions in which the miners worked and lived were slowly being improved. The coal seams close to Ayr, such as those within the fort area, and in Newton, were rapidly approaching exhaustion, and the coal companies were looking for new seams. This search led them inland, and the main sources of coal in the Ayr district in the late 19th century were around Whitletts, Coylton, Annbank and Mossblown. Most of these villages had not existed before the coming of the miners. The major coal-owner was still George Taylor & Co (the Ayr Coal Company), and in villages such as Annbank, they were responsible for providing the housing, the shops, and facilities such as the school.

For all classes there were opportunities for sport and leisure. References to horse racing in Ayr go back as far as 1576. These races were probably on the sands. In 1770 a course was laid out on the ground now known as the Old Racecourse, and this was gradually transformed into a first class and popular race-course. The best known trophy raced for here, the Ayr Gold Cup, was first competed for in 1804, and the Western Meeting, which became the hub of Ayr's autumn social calendar, was introduced in 1824. The course continued to flourish during the late 19th century, especially once the railways enabled people from Glasgow and elsewhere to attend. By the early 20th century the course itself was regarded as too cramped, and the corners too sharp. A site was acquired between Ayr and Whitletts, where a new course was laid out. This was opened in 1907, and today is one of the premier venues for racing in Scotland. The Ayr Gold Cup meeting is still the highlight of the racing year, but Ayr has also hosted the Scottish Grand National since 1966. Previously this race had been run at Bogside, near Irvine. In the 21st century Ayr racecourse boasts first-rate facilities, a full card and strong support among the racing fraternity in Scotland.

In Newton the carters, or cadgers, also held annual races, usually in August, when the carters and their horses, all dressed in

ALEXANDER STEWART'S SHOP 1939 SA000517
(Courtesy of University of St Andrews Library)

Alexander Stewart's shoe shop was next door to the Tam o' Shanter. Alexander came to Ayr from Arran, and ran this and another shop in the Sandgate for 35 years until he retired in 1947.

First Winners

The first winner of the Ayr Gold Cup, in 1804, was Chancellor, belonging to Lord Cassillis. The first winner of the Scottish Grand National, at Ayr, in 1966 was African Patrol, ridden by Johnny Leech.

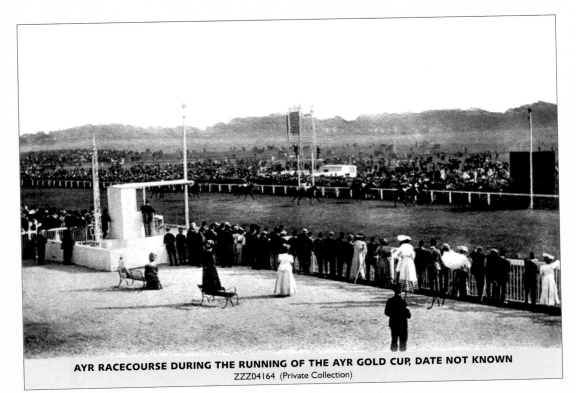

AYR RACECOURSE DURING THE RUNNING OF THE AYR GOLD CUP, DATE NOT KNOWN
ZZZ04164 (Private Collection)

their finery, took part in lively and spirited races upon the sands. The day began with a parade before the town council of Newton and finished in much hilarity, whisky and, traditionally, kippered fish. Disapproval and regulation slowly pushed the cadgers' races into obloquy and extinction.

The first recorded mention of football in Ayr is at Alloway in 1514. It was, however,

Did you know?

In September 1989 the St Leger was run at Ayr, because the course at Doncaster was unusable. The race was won by Steve Cauthen riding Michelozzo.

only in the later half of the 19th century that football, like many other codified team sports, came to resemble the game we know today. A number of teams sprang up in Ayr in the 1870s, mostly playing friendly games among themselves. The inauguration of the Ayrshire Cup in 1877, and further regular leagues and cups, both locally and nationally, gave added impetus. In 1879 Ayr Academicals and Ayr Thistle merged to become Ayr Football Club, and in 1888 this club moved to Somerset Park, where their first match was a friendly against Aston Villa, which resulted in a 3-0 home win. Soon two Ayr teams -

Ayr (admitted in 1897) and Ayr Parkhous (founded in 1886, admitted in 1903) - wer playing in the Scottish League, and in 191 they agreed to merge to create a single tean Ayr United, with greater chances of reachin the highest levels of Scottish football. Th team has been a member of the Scottis League ever since, and has remained loyal t the old ground at Somerset Park. From 196 to 1975 the 'Honest Men' were managed b the charismatic Ally McLeod, who hone at Somerset Park the skills that later mad him one the best loved football managers c Scotland's national team.

AYR UNITED'S TEAM FOR THE 1956-57 SEASON ZZZ04165 (Private Collection)

This was unfortunately not an epic season, for the team finished bottom of the First Division.

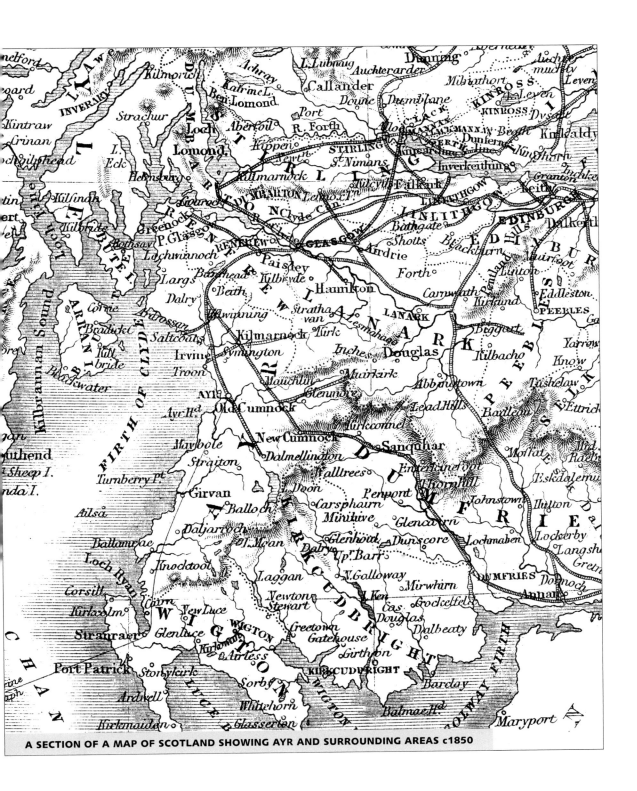

A SECTION OF A MAP OF SCOTLAND SHOWING AYR AND SURROUNDING AREAS c1850

AYR FROM THE AIR 1962   AFA102235

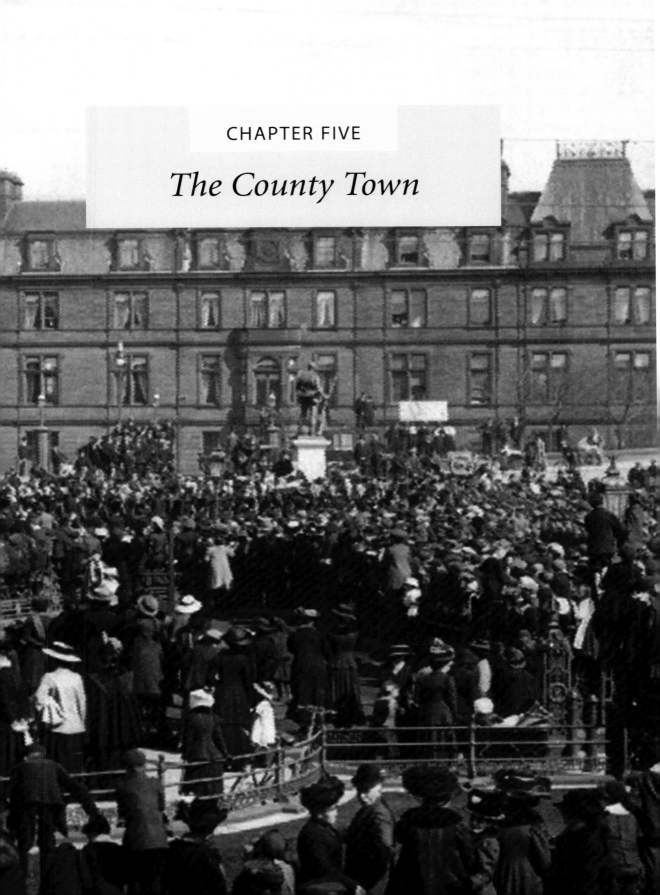

CHAPTER FIVE

The County Town

THE BURNS'S MONUMENT HOTEL 1897 39863x

DURING THE 20TH CENTURY Ayr grew steadily to become the important and flourishing commercial, residential and holiday town that it is today.

At Alloway, a museum was opened in 1900 adjacent to Burns's Cottage, which was restored to how it had looked at the time of the poet's birth. Propriety had decreed that it should no longer be a public house; the thirsty traveller was catered for by the more sophisticated Burns's Monument Hotel, which had opened in the 1830s. The cottage is still an important tourist destination, while the hotel, now named the Brig o' Doon, is one of Ayr's premier hotels, popular for weddings and other celebrations.

THE BANKS O' DOON 1926 SA000067 (Courtesy of University of St Andrews Library)

An early view of the Burns's Monument Hotel (top), and a later view of its elegant and popular tea gardens on the bank of the river Doon.

THE CROWDS AT THE FORMAL UNVEILING OF BURNS'S STATUE 1891 ZZZ04166 (Private Collection)

The attractions at Alloway were increased in the 1970s when the Tam o' Shanter Experience was first opened. This is a modern visitor attraction offering a gift shop and refreshments to the visitor, built on the site of the old Alloway railway station.

In Ayr itself the statue of Burns had been unveiled with great ceremony in 1891. The Tam o' Shanter Inn in the High Street, where Tam and his friends had got 'roaring fu' was bought by the town council and converted into a Burns's Museum, which opened in the 1950s. Thirty years later it was converted back into a pub, providing a busy and convivial focus in the High Street.

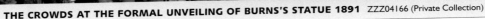

BURNS'S STATUE 1900 46008

Burns's Statue in quieter surroundings in 1900.

THE ESPLANADE 1900 45998

THE PROMENADE AND THE PAVILION 1937 SA000049 (Courtesy of University of St Andrews Library)

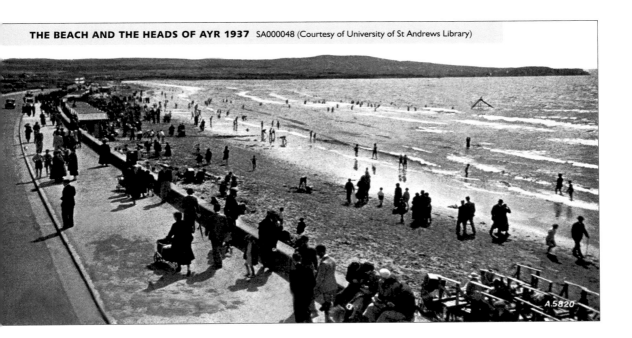

THE BEACH AND THE HEADS OF AYR 1937 SA000048 (Courtesy of University of St Andrews Library)

THE GARDENS AND THE ARRAN HILLS 1937 SA000059 (Courtesy of University of St Andrews Library)

The Esplanade photographed in 1900 (opposite, top left), while a warm summer's day in 1937 brought visitors to the beach, the Low Green and the sunken garden.

THE PROMENADE AND THE PAVILION 1937 SA000049 (Courtesy of University of St Andrews Library)

Beach holidays and sea-bathing had become increasingly popular during the 19th century. Ayr was well placed to benefit from the many thousands in Glasgow and the central belt of Scotland who wanted to spend time by the sea. The long sandy beach with its safe bathing was, and remains, very popular with all ages. Although the classic July seaside holiday now takes Scots to Spain, Greece or beyond, good summers still see Ayr beach thronged with hundreds of happy holiday-makers.

The town made improvements along the sea-shore. Most noticeable is the long Esplanade which runs from the south pier of the harbour for a couple of miles towards Seafield and Blackburn, and allowed the Victorian and Edwardian visitor the chance to promenade in style. Another was the Pavilion, opened in 1910, which was designed to host shows and other entertainments. This is one of Ayr's most attractive buildings and still survives, despite many vicissitudes. In the mid 1990s it was well known as Hanger 13, a centre of the national rave scene, and attracted some not always positive publicity. Today it is Pirate Pete's, an adventure centre for young children.

CLYDE STEAMERS c1930 ZZZ04167 (Private Collection)

Clyde Steamers were an essential part of any holiday in Ayr from the early part of the 19th century until the late 1950s. The 'Juno', which was in service from 1898 until 1931, and the 'Glen Sannox' were both regular and much-loved visitors to Ayr. Today a summer service is still provided by the preserved paddle steamer 'Waverley'.

CHARLIE KEMBLE'S SUPER ENTERTAINERS 1928   ZZZ04168 (Private Collection)

Charlie Kemble's Super Entertainers were among the acts to be seen at the Pavilion during the summer of 1928.

THE PAVILION 2005   A86722k (Rob Close)

The Gaiety Theatre

For many lovers of the stage, Ayr will always be associated with the Gaiety Theatre. This is still going strong, in Carrick Street, and is still recognised as Scotland's Home of Variety. The Gaiety Theatre was opened in 1902, and initially put on a mix of plays and light operas. In 1925 it was acquired by a Yorkshire impresario called Ben Popplewell, who had previously run the Pavilion for the town council. Ben transformed it into a variety theatre, bringing in comedians, singers, revue acts and much more. The character of the Gaiety is encapsulated in the world-famous 'Gaiety Whirls', which run throughout the summer season, offering locals and holiday-makers a first class mixture of song, humour, dance and magic.

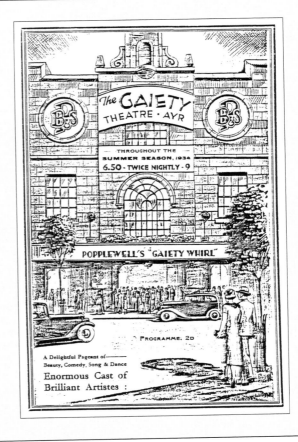

THE GAIETY THEATRE POSTER ZZZ04169
(Courtesy of South Ayrshire Libraries)

For many visitors to Ayr, the main attraction is the golf. The Ayrshire coast is one of the best places in the world to play golf. The game has been played in the county since at least the 18th century, and became increasingly popular during the 19th century. One of the first clubs to be formed was that at Prestwick, and here the first Open was competed for in 1860. Old Prestwick is now too small to host the multi-million pound event that the Open has become, but two Ayrshire courses, Royal Troon and Turnberry, are regular venues.

THE MONUMENT MARKING THE SITE OF THE FIRST TEE AT THE FIRST OPEN IN 1860 2005 A86723k (Rob Close)

THE ICE RINK 1939 SA000053 (Courtesy of University of St Andrews Library)

BURNS'S STATUE SQUARE 1938 SA000051 (Courtesy of University of St Andrews Library)

The brand new Odeon Cinema dominates Burns's Statue Square in this view from 1938.

Other leisure facilities included cinemas. At one time Ayr had half-a-dozen or so cinemas, including the Orient in Newton, which was most recently a nightclub, and Green's Playhouse, which is now a busy bingo hall. The only surviving cinema is the Odeon, which was opened in 1936, and now has four screens showing a changing programme of modern films. Close to the Odeon was the original Ayr ice rink, built during the height of the ice skating craze. It was closed, and the site converted into a supermarket, and a new ice rink built in Newton. This is still a busy venue for skating, ice hockey and curling.

Did you know?
Frank Sinatra

On 12 July 1953 Frank Sinatra appeared at Green's Playhouse. The local press reported that the world-famous crooner, who was in Ayr because of the large American presence at Prestwick Airport, gave 'one of the most informal performances of his career.'

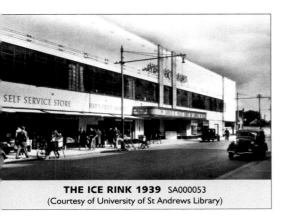

THE ICE RINK 1939 SA000053
(Courtesy of University of St Andrews Library)

The original Ayr ice rink, photographed shortly after it opened in March 1939. Hay's smart modern grocery store, with the novelty of 'self service', survived until 1962, and the ice rink itself was demolished in 1972.

Ayr and the surrounding towns and villages were caught up in the wars that punctuated the 20th century. A statue in Burns's Statue Square is a memorial to the men of the county, and particularly of the county regiment, the Royal Scots Fusiliers, who died while fighting in the Boer Wars. During the Great War (as the First World War was known), again, many men from Ayr fought and died for their country, and they are commemorated by the cenotaph in Wellington Square. The Clyde estuary was an important naval centre, while the area was also home to some of the earliest experiments with military aircraft. A squadron of the Royal Flying Corps, many of whom were Newfoundlanders, was based at Turnberry, where there is a monument to them, close to the lighthouse and remains of Bruce's castle. Inland, at Loch Doon, much money was spent on the development of an aerial bombing school, and some relics of this can still be seen.

Ayr's first holder of the Victoria Cross was Lieutenant Robert Shankland of the Canadian Cameron Highlanders. Robert had been born in Wallacetown, and had attended Smith's Institution before emigrating to Canada. He won his VC for his bravery during the Battle of Passchendaele in 1915.

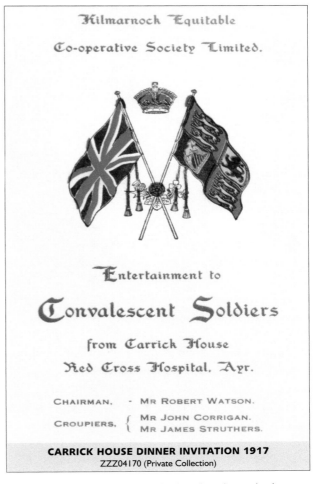

CARRICK HOUSE DINNER INVITATION 1917
ZZZ04170 (Private Collection)

Military hospitals were established in Ayr during both wars. During the Great War one such was at Carrick House, and the soldiers convalescing there were treated to this dinner and entertainment in April 1917.

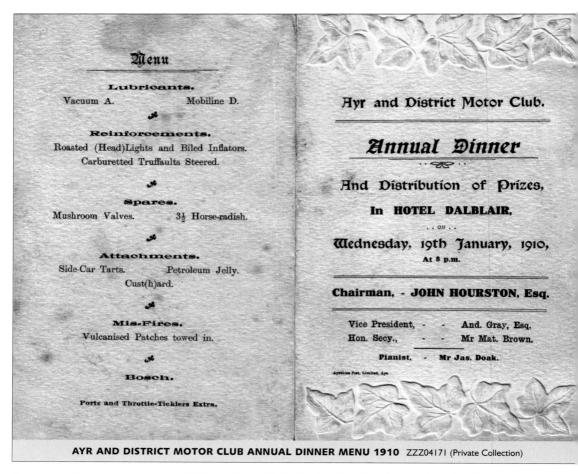

Menu

Lubricants.

Vacuum A.   Mobiline D.

Reinforcements.

Roasted (Head)Lights and Biled Inflators.
Carburetted Truffaults Steered.

Spares.

Mushroom Valves.   3½ Horse-radish.

Attachments.

Side-Car Tarts.   Petroleum Jelly.
Cust(h)ard.

Mis-Fires.

Vulcanised Patches towed in.

Bosch.

Ports and Throttle-Ticklers Extra.

Ayr and District Motor Club.

Annual Dinner

And Distribution of Prizes,

In HOTEL DALBLAIR,

.. ON ..

Wednesday, 19th January, 1910,

At 8 p.m.

Chairman, - JOHN HOURSTON, Esq.

Vice President, - - And. Gray, Esq.
Hon. Secy., - - Mr Mat. Brown.

Pianist, - Mr Jas. Doak.

Ayrshire Post, Limited, Ayr

AYR AND DISTRICT MOTOR CLUB ANNUAL DINNER MENU 1910 ZZZ04171 (Private Collection)

Early motorists, such as the Ayr and District Motor Club, clearly enjoyed both a good meal and a good joke.

The most noticeable change in Ayr between the wars was in the growth of the private car. As cars became more reliable, and cheaper, more and more people took to the joys of motoring. One result of this was that people could live further from their work, so that the town began to spread, as new houses, with gardens and garages, appeared on the edges, especially on the south and east, and around existing small settlements such as Alloway. The adven of the car helped to speed the end of Ayr' tramway system. This had begun in 1901 and had lines linking Prestwick, Alloway and the New Racecourse. It was closed in 1932, though brackets for the wires can stil be seen on some buildings in the town.

The car also encouraged the developmen of the road-house, where motorists could get refreshments in modern and stylish surroundings. A well-known local road-house was the Dutch House, found on the Glasgow road beyond Monkton. This still survives, though much altered, as the heart of a caravan site. The car also made it easier for visitors to, and residents of, Ayr to get to local tourist attractions such as Culzean Castle, which had been gifted to the National Trust for Scotland by the Kennedy family and opened to the public in 1954.

Ayr played its part in the Second World War. The Clyde, again, was an important naval base, with many local mansions requisitioned for military purposes. The barracks of the Royal Scots Fusiliers were near the current Citadel Leisure Centre, and have now been replaced by modern housing. One street name here - Donnini Court - commemorates Dennis Donnini from County Durham, who was awarded a posthumous VC for his bravery in the Netherlands while serving with the Royal Scots Fusiliers in 1945.

The entrepreneur Billy Butlin had made plans for a holiday camp near Ayr before the Second World War. During the war his site was taken over by the government and run as a signalling training centre, HMS 'Scotia'. After the war, it was returned to Butlin, and Butlin's Ayr quickly became a popular holiday destination. Now called Craig Tara, it still offers a wide range of facilities, and remains a busy and important part of Ayr's tourist industry.

The estate of Ballochmyle, near Mauchline, became a large military hospital, while Turnberry Hotel was taken over for military intelligence. Here many plans were hatched, including those for the Normandy Invasion. The American president, Dwight Eisenhower, was a frequent visitor and stayed at Culzean Castle. Ayr's and Ayrshire's importance during this war was due to their distance from enemy lines, and thus their relative security from bombing raids. The major factor however was Prestwick Airport.

Donald McIntyre was one of the pioneers of aviation. With the Marquis of Clydesdale, he had been the first person to fly over Mount Everest. McIntyre could see the commercial possibilities of flying. McIntyre's guidance and enthusiasm turned the grass landing strip at Prestwick, first made in the 1930s, into a fully-fledged airport by the outbreak of the Second World War. Once America had entered the war, Prestwick became an important link in connections between the two countries. American troops and American equipment were flown into western Europe through Prestwick, and made Ayrshire the ideal venue for transatlantic discussions.

After the war, Prestwick was developed further. Initially it became an important American base, and the runways were lengthened to take the biggest planes. At the same time Scottish Aviation Ltd (McIntyre's company) began to build planes at Prestwick. They had started during the war, using the Palace of Engineering which had been moved to the airport from the 1938 Exhibition in Glasgow. Prestwick also began to develop commercial flights.

The presence of American troops brought to 1950s Ayr a vibrancy which, whilst not always welcomed, helped Ayr to support, for a few years, a successful ice hockey team, the Ayr Bruins.

After some lean times, especially after the American troops were withdrawn, Prestwick Airport has now become a busy and growing hub, especially for one of Britain's leading low-cost airlines, which offers daily flights from Prestwick to many places in western Europe.

Did you know?
Elvis Presley

Elvis Presley rarely travelled outside the United States, and he never performed a concert in Britain. However while returning from his military service in West Germany, the Douglas DC7 he was on stopped to refuel at Prestwick Airport, with the result that on 2 March 1960 Prestwick witnessed his only (and brief) appearance on British soil.

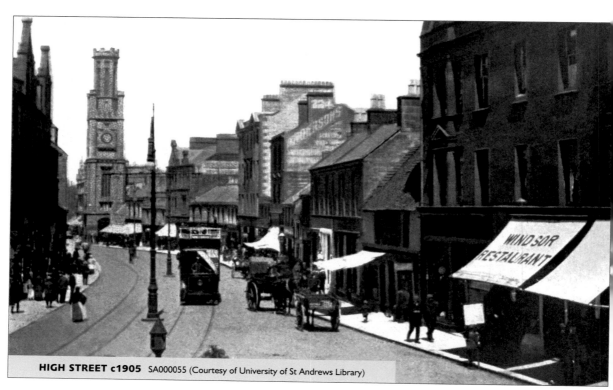

HIGH STREET c1905 SA000055 (Courtesy of University of St Andrews Library)

An Ayr Corporation tram makes its way sedately up the High Street. Pierre Andreoli, who had been the head waiter at the Station Hotel, ran the Windsor Restaurant 'in a way that has always been favourably commented upon', from 1903 until 1922, when he moved across the road to Goudie's Restaurant. An Italian by birth, his naturalisation papers were signed by Winston Churchill.

HIGH STREET 1900 46002v

The High Street in 1900. John Wallace's drapery business in Victoria House lasted from 1897 until the early 1900s, when it was taken over by Anderson Brothers.

LITTLEJOHN BROTHERS ADVERTISEMENT ZZZ04172
(Private Collection)

LITTLEJOHN BROTHERS ADVERTISEMENT
ZZZ04173 (Private Collection)

The Littlejohn Brothers began as wine merchants in 1818. The business expanded to include their own brands of whisky and port. Their shop in the Sandgate is still an off-licence.

The 20th century has seen a tremendous growth in shopping and the retail business. Once a necessity, it is now a leisure activity. Ayr's main shopping streets have always been the High Street and Sandgate, together with Newmarket Street and Alloway Street, while the Main Street of Newton has always been important north of the river. These streets have remained the heart of the town, though they have changed in appearance. Most of the 18th century shops, with houses above, have now gone, replaced by modern shops. During the 1930s Woolworths replaced the Kings Arms, which had been the main coaching inn for the town, and new shops in a similar 1930s style were also built at this end of the High Street for Montagu Burton (now the Rangers Shop) and Marks and Spencer (now the Forum). Ayr's first department store had appeared in 1896 when David Hourston opened his premises in Alloway Street, and this was greatly extended in 1910.

Redevelopment continued anew from the 1960s, with new shopping centres such as Dalblair Arcade (now Arran Mall, opened in 1967) and the Kyle Centre (completed in 1988). Major stores were redeveloped such as Littlewoods (opened in 1969, and replacing both John Welch's Garden and the Gaumont Cinema), Marks and Spencer (opened in 1974, replacing the last medieval house in the High Street) and British Home Stores (1983). The downside of this has been the loss of the small, local trader. In the town centre, it is probable that only A Picken & Sons, butchers (1870) and Wallace Allan, jeweller (1872) can trace their history back before 1900.

Stephen & Pollock

STEPHEN & POLLOCK
37, Sandgate & 68, Newmarket Street,
AYR.

A STEPHEN & POLLOCK BOOKMARK ZZZ04174 (Private Collection)

A local business which has now gone was that of Stephen & Pollock, booksellers. Hugh Pollock, son of the founder, became a book editor in London, where he met and married a young writer for children, called Enid Blyton. Although the marriage eventually broke down, the creator of Noddy, the Famous Five and other adventure stories for children was an occasional visitor to Ayr.

The 1990s saw the growth of out-of-town shopping, and Ayr's biggest centre of this type, at Heathfield, was opened in 1994. The development is called Liberator Way, after the American aircraft type which was a mainstay of the wartime links between Great Britain and America.

In 2005 Ayr celebrates the 800th anniversary of its creation as a royal burgh. It goes forward in good spirit. Ayr is recognised as a good place to live, with good shopping and employment bases, and many attractive residential areas. It boasts good transport links, especially through Prestwick Airport, and the opening of the M77 in April 2005 has further improved its connections. It has good educational facilities, with opportunities for higher education at the Scottish Agricultural College at Auchincruive, at the Craigie Campus of the University of Paisley, and at Ayr College.

A new shopping development is being built on the site of Templetons Mill in Kyle Street, which will increase the town's attractiveness as a commercial centre, while the proposed new development at the racecourse will increase both its commercial and leisure aspects, bringing to the town its first multiplex cinema. The bowling greens at Northfield, which have been steadily developed over the last 20 years, are now regarded as the unofficial home of bowling in Scotland, and attract thousands of visitors to the town each year for the various national and international competitions. The annual Ayr Flower Show is one of the highlights of the horticultural year in Scotland, while the Ayr Agricultural Show, and the lively Cattle Market, indicate Ayr's importance to the thriving agricultural industry in the county.

Development of the sea front has not been neglected. The new housing on the south harbour side has breathed new life into a neglected part of the town, while the adjacent Citadel Leisure Centre provides a wealth of opportunities for sport and leisure. The port itself, though no longer home to the fishing fleet, is still busy, with ships coming and going, bringing logs and still taking coal. The paddle steamer 'Waverley' appears every summer, while the occasional cruise liner dwarfs everything.

The unique Millennium Bridge at Doonfoot has been designed as part of the local cycleway network, and also allows people to extend the walk along the Esplanade as far as the mouth of the River Doon and on towards Greenan Castle. The bridge is the most noticeable and lasting memorial of Ayr's millennium celebrations. Also on the Esplanade, a Lang Scots Mile has been designated, with appropriate signs, to encourage people to walk more and improve their fitness. These walks supplement the older River Ayr Walk which runs along the River Ayr from the centre of the town out to the by-pass and on to Auchincruive. There are current plans to extend this walk further upstream.

Ayr remains an important administrative centre, with the offices of South Ayrshire Council and other government offices. It has a strong employment base, and is also well situated for commuters to Glasgow and Paisley. Prestwick Airport provides further employment, and there are a number of associated businesses at the airport and at the adjacent business park. The strong tourist industry also contributes greatly to Ayr's commercial success.

Ayr goes forward into its ninth century in good heart. It has an unrivalled setting, excellent facilities and a proud and committed population who are determined to ensure that it remains one of the most attractive places in Scotland in which to live.

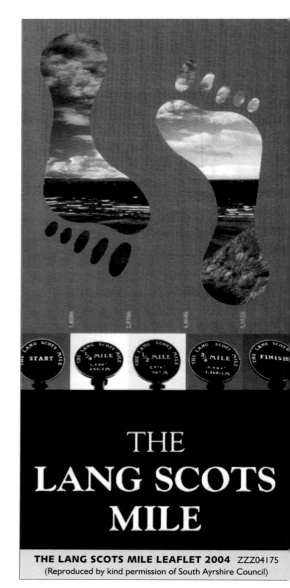

THE LANG SCOTS MILE LEAFLET 2004 ZZZ04175
(Reproduced by kind permission of South Ayrshire Council)

ACKNOWLEDGEMENTS AND FURTHER READING

This book is a result of many years rooting about in the history of Ayr. Many people have helped along the way, sharing their time, their knowledge and their thoughts; they include Sheena and the late Ken Andrew, the late John Strawhorn, Alastair Hendry, Rob Urquhart, Michael Hitchon, David McClure, and all past and present members of the ever helpful Local History Library (especially Tom, Sheila and Sheena) and Ayrshire Archives (especially Kevin, Christine, Pamela, and Marion). I am also indebted to my colleagues in the Civic Society and the Archaeological Society. For this book particular thanks are due to Dane Love, Jean Kennedy, Rosalind Smith, Tom Barclay, Anne Joel and the Managing Editor at The Francis Frith Collection, Julia Skinner. Geordies Byre keeps me in touch with the 21st century. Joy Gladstone continues to tolerate and encourage my interests and ambitions.

The primary source for anyone wishing to delve further into Ayr's history is John Strawhorn's 'The History of Ayr' (Edinburgh, 1989), which also contains a comprehensive bibliography. The other definitive book on Ayr is that edited by Annie Dunlop, 'The Royal Burgh of Ayr' (Ayr, 1953). Also of use are 'Historic Ayr' and 'Historic Alloway', both published jointly by the Ayrshire Archaeological and Natural History Society and the Kyle and Carrick Civic Society (2001, 2000), Dane Love's 'Ayr Stories' (Ayr, 2000), Lindsay and Kennedy's 'The Burgesses and Guild Brethren of Ayr 1647-1846' (Ayr, 2002) and my 'The Street Names of Ayr' (Ayr, 2001). For Prestwick, John Strawhorn's 'The History of Prestwick' (Edinburgh, 1994) should be the first port of call.

Photographs used by courtesy of University of St Andrews Library are reproduced from digital copies of the originals held in the University of St Andrews Library. For further information about the collections, obtaining copies of images, or authorisation to reproduce them, please refer to http://specialcollections.st-and.ac.uk, or contact Department of Special Collections, University of St Andrews Library, North Street, St Andrews, Fife KY16 9TR (tel 01334-462339; email speccoll@st-and.ac.uk).

Francis Frith
Pioneer Victorian Photographer

Francis Frith, founder of the world-famous photographic archive, was a multi-talented man. A devout Quaker and a highly successful Victorian businessman, he was philosophical by nature and pioneering in outlook. By 1855 he had already established a wholesale grocery business in Liverpool, and sold it for the astonishing sum of £200,000, which is the equivalent today of over £15,000,000. Now in his thirties, and captivated by the new science of photography, Frith set out on a series of pioneering journeys up the Nile and to the Near East.

He was the first photographer to venture beyond the sixth cataract of the Nile. Africa was still the mysterious 'Dark Continent', and Stanley and Livingstone's historic meeting was a decade into the future. The conditions for picture taking confound belief. He laboured for hours in his wicker dark-room in the sweltering heat of the desert, while the volatile chemicals fizzed dangerously in their trays. Back in London he exhibited his photographs and was 'rapturously cheered' by members of the Royal Society. His reputation as a photographer was made overnight.

By the 1870s the railways had threaded their way across the country, and Bank Holidays and half-day Saturdays had been made obligatory by Act of Parliament. All of a sudden the working man and his family were able to enjoy days out, take holidays, and see a little more of the world.

With typical business acumen, Francis Frith foresaw that these new tourists would enjoy having souvenirs to commemorate their days out. For the next thirty years he travelled the country by train and by pony and trap, producing fine photographs of seaside resorts and beauty spots that were keenly bought by millions of Victorians. These prints were painstakingly pasted into family albums and pored over during the dark nights of winter, rekindling precious memories of summer excursions. Frith's studio was soon supplying retail shops all over the country, and by 1890 F Frith & Co had become the greatest specialist photographic publishing company in the world, with over 2,000 sales outlets, and pioneered the picture postcard.

Francis Frith had died in 1898 at his villa in Cannes, his great project still growing. By 1970 the archive he created contained over a third of a million pictures showing 7,000 British towns and villages.

Frith's legacy to us today is of immense significance and value, for the magnificent archive of evocative photographs he created provides a unique record of change in the cities, towns and villages throughout Britain over a century and more. Frith and his fellow studio photographers revisited locations many times down the years to update their views, compiling for us an enthralling and colourful pageant of British life and character.

We are fortunate that Frith was dedicated to recording the minutiae of everyday life. For it is this sheer wealth of visual data, the painstaking chronicle of changes in dress, transport, street layouts, buildings, housing and landscape that captivates us so much today, offering us a powerful link with the past and with the lives of our ancestors.

Computers have now made it possible for Frith's many thousands of images to be accessed almost instantly. The archive offers every one of us an opportunity to examine the places where we and our families have lived and worked down the years. Its images, depicting our shared past, are now bringing pleasure and enlightenment to millions around the world a century and more after his death. For further information visit: **www.francisfrith.com**

FRITH PRODUCTS & SERVICES

Francis Frith would doubtless be pleased to know that the pioneering publishing venture he started in 1860 still continues today. Over a hundred and forty years later, The Francis Frith Collection continues in the same innovative tradition and is now one of the foremost publishers of vintage photographs in the world. Some of the current activities include:

INTERIOR DECORATION

Today Frith's photographs can be seen framed and as giant wall murals in thousands of pubs, restaurants, hotels, banks, retail stores and other public buildings throughout the country. In every case they enhance the unique local atmosphere of the places they depict and provide reminders of gentler days in an increasingly busy and frenetic world.

PRODUCT PROMOTIONS

Frith products are used by many major companies to promote the sales of their own products or to reinforce their own history and heritage. Frith promotions have been used by Hovis bread, Courage beers, Scots Porage Oats, Colman's mustard, Cadbury's foods, Mellow Birds coffee, Dunhill pipe tobacco, Guinness, and Bulmer's Cider.

GENEALOGY AND FAMILY HISTORY

As the interest in family history and roots grows world-wide, more and more people are turning to Frith's photographs of Great Britain for images of the towns, villages and streets where their ancestors lived; and, of course, photographs of the churches and chapels where their ancestors were christened, married and buried are an essential part of every genealogy tree and family album.

FRITH PRODUCTS

All Frith photographs are available Framed or just as Mounted Prints and unmounted versions. These may be ordered from the address below. Other products available are - Calendars, Jigsaws, Canvas Prints, Mugs, Tea Towels, Tableware and local and prestige books.

THE INTERNET

Over several hundred thousand Frith photographs can be viewed and purchased on the internet through the Frith websites!

For more detailed information on Frith products, look at **www.francisfrith.com**

See the complete list of Frith Books at: www.francisfrith.com
This web site is regularly updated with the latest list of publications from The Francis Frith Collection. If you wish to buy books relating to another part of the country that your local bookshop does not stock, you may purchase on-line.

For further information, trade, or author enquiries please contact us at the address below:
The Francis Frith Collection, Unit 19 Kingsmead Business Park, Gillingham, Dorset SP8 5FB.
Tel: +44 (0)1722 716 376   Email: sales@francisfrith.co.uk

See Frith products on the internet at www.francisfrith.com

FREE PRINT OF YOUR CHOICE
CHOOSE A PHOTOGRAPH FROM THIS BOOK
+ POSTAGE

Mounted Print
Overall size 14 x 11 inches (355 x 280mm)

TO RECEIVE YOUR FREE PRINT

Choose any Frith photograph in this book

Simply complete the Voucher opposite and return it with your payment (to cover postage and handling) and we will print the photograph of your choice in SEPIA (size 11 x 8 inches) and supply it in a cream mount ready to frame (overall size 14 x 11 inches).

Order additional Mounted Prints at HALF PRICE - £19.00 each (normally £38.00)

If you would like to order more Frith prints from this book, possibly as gifts for friends and family, you can buy them at half price (with no additional postage costs).

Have your Mounted Prints framed

For an extra £20.00 per print you can have your mounted print(s) framed in an elegant polished wood and gilt moulding, overall size 16 x 13 inches (no additional postage required).

IMPORTANT!

❶ Please note: aerial photographs and photographs with a reference number starting with a "Z" are not Frith photographs and cannot be supplied under this offer.

❷ Offer valid for delivery to one UK address only.

❸ These special prices are only available if you use this form to order. You must use the ORIGINAL VOUCHER on this page (no copies permitted). We can only despatch to one UK address.

❹ This offer cannot be combined with any other offer.

As a customer your name & address will be stored by Frith but not sold or rented to third parties. Your data will be used for the purpose of this promotion only.

Send completed Voucher form to:

**The Francis Frith Collection,
19 Kingsmead Business Park, Gillingham,
Dorset SP8 5FB**

Voucher for **FREE** and Reduced Price Frith Prints

Please do not photocopy this voucher. Only the original is valid, so please fill it in, cut it out and return it to us with your order.

Picture ref no	Page no	Qty	Mounted @ £19.00	Framed + £20.00	Total Cost £
		1	Free of charge*	£	£
			£19.00	£	£
			£19.00	£	£
			£19.00	£	£
			£19.00	£	£
			£19.00	£	£

*Please allow 28 days for delivery.
Offer available to one UK address only*

* Post & handling	£3.80
Total Order Cost	£

Title of this book . . . .

I enclose a cheque/postal order for £ . . . .
made payable to 'The Francis Frith Collection'

OR please debit my Mastercard / Visa / Maestro card, details below

Card Number:

Issue No (Maestro only):   Valid from (Maestro):

Card Security Number: Expires:

Signature:

Name Mr/Mrs/Ms . . . .

Address . . . .

. . . .

. . . .

. . . . Postcode . . . .

Daytime Tel No . . . .

Email . . . .

Valid to 31/12/20

Free Print – see overleaf

Can you help us with information about any of the Frith photographs in this book?

We are gradually compiling an historical record for each of the photographs in the Frith archive. It is always fascinating to find out the names of the people shown in the pictures, as well as insights into the shops, buildings and other features depicted.

If you recognize anyone in the photographs in this book, or if you have information not already included in the author's caption, do let us know. We would love to hear from you, and will try to publish it in future books or articles.

An Invitation from The Francis Frith Collection to Share Your Memories

The 'Share Your Memories' feature of our website allows members of the public to add personal memories relating to the places featured in our photographs, or comment on others already added. Seeing a place from your past can rekindle forgotten or long held memories. Why not visit the website, find photographs of places you know well and add YOUR story for others to read and enjoy? We would love to hear from you!

www.francisfrith.com/memories

Our production team

Frith books are produced by a small dedicated team at offices near Salisbury. Most have worked with the Frith Collection for many years. All have in common one quality: they have a passion for the Frith Collection.

Frith Books and Gifts

We have a wide range of books and gifts available on our website utilising our photographic archive, many of which can be individually personalised.

www.francisfrith.com